242

D1785471

MOSCOW

THE WORLD 100 YEARS AGO

THE WORLD 100 YEARS AGO

BURTON HOLMES

MOSCOW

FRED L. ISRAEL
General Editor

ARTHUR M. SCHLESINGER, JR.
Senior Consulting Editor

CHELSEA HOUSE PUBLISHERS
Philadelphia

CHELSEA HOUSE PUBLISHERS

EDITOR-IN-CHIEF Stephen Reginald
MANAGING EDITOR James D. Gallagher
PRODUCTION MANAGER Pamela Loos
ART DIRECTOR Sara Davis
PICTURE EDITOR Judy Hasday
SENIOR PRODUCTION EDITOR Lisa Chippendale
ASSOCIATE ART DIRECTOR Takeshi Takahashi
COVER DESIGN Dave Loose Design

First Printing

1 3 5 7 9 8 6 4 2

Library of Congress Cataloging-in-Publication Data

Holmes, Burton, b. 1870.
Moscow/ Burton Holmes; Fred L. Israel, general editor;
Arthur M. Schlesinger, jr., senior consulting editor.
  p. cm. —(World 100 years ago)
Includes index.

ISBN 0-7910-4658-3 (hc) ISBN 0-7910-4659-1 (pb).

1. Moscow (Russia)—Description and travel. 2. Holmes,
Burton, b. 1870—Journeys—Russia (Federation)—
Moscow. I. Israel, Fred L. II. Schlesinger, Arthur Meier,
1917- . III. Title. IV. Series: Holmes, Burton, b. 1870.
World 100 years ago today.
DK601.2.H65   1997
914.704'83—dc21   97-29395
                                                            CIP
                                                            r97

CONTENTS

The Great Globe Trotter

By Irving Wallace

One day in the year 1890, Miss Nellie Bly, of the *New York World,* came roaring into Brooklyn on a special train from San Francisco. In a successful effort to beat Phileas Fogg's fictional 80 days around the world, Miss Bly, traveling with two handbags and flannel underwear, had circled the globe in 72 days, 6 hours, and 11 minutes. Immortality awaited her.

Elsewhere that same year, another less-publicized globe-girdler made his start toward immortality. He was Mr. Burton Holmes, making his public debut with slides and anecdotes ("Through Europe With a Kodak") before the Chicago Camera Club. Mr. Holmes, while less spectacular than his feminine rival, was destined, for that very reason, soon to dethrone her as America's number-one traveler.

Today, Miss Bly and Mr. Holmes have one thing in common: In the mass mind they are legendary vagabonds relegated to the dim and dusty past of the Iron Horse and the paddle-wheel steamer. But if Miss Bly, who shuffled off this mortal coil in 1922, is now only a part of our folklore, there are millions to testify that

Mr. Burton Holmes, aged seventy-six, is still very much with us.

Remembering that Mr. Holmes was an active contemporary of Miss Bly's, that he was making a livelihood at traveling when William McKinley, John L. Sullivan, and Admiral Dewey ruled the United States, when Tony Pastor, Lily Langtry, and Lillian Russell ruled the amusement world, it is at once amazing and reassuring to pick up the daily newspapers of 1946 and find, sandwiched between advertisements of rash young men lecturing on "Inside Stalin" and "I Was Hitler's Dentist," calm announcements that tomorrow evening Mr. Burton Holmes has something more to say about "Beautiful Bali."

Burton Holmes, a brisk, immaculate, chunky man with gray Vandyke beard, erect bearing, precise speech ("folks are always mistaking me for Monty Woolley," he says, not unhappily), is one of the seven wonders of the entertainment world. As Everyman's tourist, Burton Holmes has crossed the Atlantic Ocean thirty times, the Pacific Ocean twenty times, and has gone completely around the world six times. He has spent fifty-five summers abroad, and recorded a half million feet of film of those summers. He was the first person to take motion picture cameras into Russia and Japan. He witnessed the regular decennial performance of the Passion Play at Oberammergau in 1890, and attended the first modern Olympics at Athens in 1896. He rode on the first Trans-Siberian train across Russia, and photographed the world's first airplane meet at Rheims.

As the fruit of these travels, Burton Holmes has delivered approximately 8,000 illustrated lectures that have grossed, according to an estimate by *Variety,* five million dollars in fifty-three winters. Because he does not like to be called a lecturer— "I'm a performer," he insists, "and I have performed on more legitimate stages than platforms"—he invented the word "travelogue" in London to describe his activity.

His travelogues, regarded as a fifth season of the year in most communities, have won him such popularity that he holds the record for playing in the longest one-man run in American show business. In the five and a half decades past, Burton Holmes has successively met the hectic competition of big-time vaudeville, stage, silent pictures, radio, and talking pictures, and he has survived them all.

At an age when most men have retired to slippered ease or are hounded by high blood pressure, Burton Holmes is more active and more popular than ever before. In the season just finished, which he started in San Francisco during September, 1945, and wound up in New York during April, 1946, Holmes appeared in 187 shows, a record number. He averaged six travelogues a week, spoke for two hours at each, and did 30 percent more box-office business than five years ago. Not once was a scheduled lecture postponed or canceled. In fact, he has missed only two in his life. In 1935, flying over the Dust Bowl, he suffered laryngitis and was forced to bypass two college dates. He has never canceled an appearance before a paid city audience. Seven years ago, when one of his elderly limbs was fractured in an automobile crack-up in Finland, there was a feeling that Burton Holmes might not make the rounds. When news of the accident was released, it was as if word had gone out that Santa Claus was about to cancel his winter schedule. But when the 1939 season dawned, Burton Holmes rolled on the stage in a wheelchair, and from his seat of pain (and for 129 consecutive appearances thereafter), he delivered his travel chat while 16-mm film shimmered on the screen beside him.

Today, there is little likelihood that anything, except utter extinction, could keep Holmes from his waiting audiences. Even now, between seasons, Holmes is in training for his next series— 150 illustrated lectures before groups in seventeen states.

Before World War II, accompanied by Margaret Oliver, his wife of thirty-two years, Holmes would spend his breathing spells on summery excursions through the Far East or Europe. While aides captured scenery on celluloid, Holmes wrote accompanying lecture material in his notebooks. Months later, he would communicate his findings to his cult, at a maximum price of $1.50 per seat. With the outbreak of war, Holmes changed his pattern. He curtailed travel outside the Americas. This year, except for one journey to Las Vegas, Nevada, where he personally photographed cowboy cutups and shapely starlets at the annual Helldorado festival, Holmes has been allowing his assistants to do all his traveling for him.

Recently, one crew, under cameraman Thayer Soule, who helped shoot the Battle of Tarawa for the Marines, brought Holmes a harvest of new film from Mexico. Another crew, after four months in Brazil last year, and two in its capital this year, returned to Holmes with magnificent movies. Meantime, other crews, under assignment from Holmes, are finishing films on Death Valley, the West Indies, and the Mississippi River.

In a cottage behind his sprawling Hollywood hilltop home, Holmes is busy, day and night, sorting the incoming negative, cutting and editing it, and rewriting lectures that will accompany the footage this winter. He is too busy to plan his next trip. Moreover, he doesn't feel that he should revisit Europe yet. "I wouldn't mind seeing it," he says, "but I don't think my public would be interested. My people want a good time, they want escape, they want sweetness and light, beauty and charm. There is too much rubble and misery over there now, and I'll let those picture magazines and Fox Movietone newsreels show all that. I'll wait until it's tourist time again."

When he travels, he thinks he will visit three of the four accessible places on earth that he has not yet seen. One is Tahiti, which he barely missed a dozen times, and the other two are Iran and Iraq. The remaining country that he has not seen, and has no wish to see, is primitive Afghanistan. Of all cities on earth, he would most like to revisit Kyoto, once capital of Japan. He still recalls that the first movies ever made inside Japan were ones he made in Kyoto, in 1899. The other cities he desires to revisit are

Venice and Rome. The only island for which he has any longing is Bali—"the one quaint spot on earth where you can really get away from it all."

In preparing future subjects, Holmes carefully studies the success of his past performances. Last season, his two most popular lectures in the East were "California" and "Adventures in Mexico." The former grossed $5,100 in two Chicago shows; the latter jammed the St. Louis Civic Auditorium with thirty-five hundred potential señores and señoritas. Holmes will use these subjects again, with revisions, next season, and add some brand-new Latin American and United States topics. He will sidestep anything relating to war. He feels, for example, that anything dealing with the once exotic Pacific islands might have a questionable reception—"people will still remember those white crosses they saw in newsreels of Guadalcanal and Iwo Jima."

Every season presents its own obstacles, and the next will challenge Holmes with a new audience of travel-sated and disillusioned ex-GI's. Many of these men, and their families, now know that a South Sea island paradise means mosquitoes and malaria and not Melville's Fayaway and Loti's Rarahu. They know Europe means mud and ruins and not romance. Nevertheless, Holmes is confident that he will win these people over.

"The veterans of World War II will come to my travelogues just as their fathers did. After the First World War, I gave illustrated lectures on the sights of France, and the ex-doughboys enjoyed them immensely. But I suppose there's no use comparing that war to this. The First World War was a minor dispute between gentlemen. In this one, the atrocities and miseries will be difficult to forget. I know I can't give my Beautiful Italy lecture next season to men who know Italy only as a pigsty, but you see, in my heart Italy is forever beautiful, and I see things in Italy they can't see, poor fellows. How could they? . . . Still, memory is frail, and one day these boys will forget and come to my lectures not to hoot but to relive the better moments and enjoy themselves."

While Burton Holmes prepares his forthcoming shows, his business manager, a slightly built dynamo named Walter Everest, works on next season's bookings. Everest contacts organizations interested in sponsoring a lecture series, arranges dates and prices, and often leases auditoriums on his own. Everest concentrates on cities where Holmes is known to be popular, Standing Room Only cities like New York, Boston, Philadelphia, Chicago, Los Angeles. On the other hand, he is cautious about the cities where Holmes has been unpopular in the past—Toledo, Cleveland, Indianapolis, Cincinnati. The one city Holmes now avoids entirely is Pomona, California, where, at a scheduled Saturday matinee, he found himself facing an almost empty house. The phenomenon of a good city or a poor city is inexplicable. In rare cases, there may be a reason for failure, and then Holmes will attempt to resolve it. When San Francisco was stone-deaf to Holmes, investigation showed that he had been competing with the annual opera season. Last year, he rented a theater the week before the opera began. He appeared eight times and made a handsome profit.

Once Holmes takes to the road for his regular season, he is a perpetual-motion machine. Leaving his wife behind, he barnstorms with his manager, Everest, and a projectionist, whirling to Western dates in his Cadillac, making long hops by plane, following the heavier Eastern circuit by train. Holmes likes to amaze younger men with his activities during a typical week. If he speaks in Detroit on a Tuesday night, he will lecture in Chicago on Wednesday evening, in Milwaukee on Thursday, be back in Chicago for Friday evening and a Saturday matinee session, then go on to Kansas City on Sunday, St. Louis on Monday, and play a return engagement in Detroit on Tuesday.

This relentless merry-go-round (with Saturday nights off to attend a newsreel "and see what's happening in the world") invigorates Holmes, but grinds his colleagues to a frazzle. One morning last season, after weeks of trains and travel, Walter

Everest was awakened by a porter at six. He rose groggily, sat swaying on the edge of his berth trying to put on his shoes. He had the look of a man who had pushed through the Matto Grosso on foot. He glanced up sleepily, and there, across the aisle, was Holmes, fully dressed, looking natty and refreshed. Holmes smiled sympathetically. "I know, Walter," he said, "this life is tiring. One day both of us ought to climb on some train and get away from it all."

In his years on the road, Holmes has come to know his audience thoroughly. He is firm in the belief that it is composed mostly of traveled persons who wish to savor the glamorous sights of the world again. Through Burton, they relive their own tours. Of the others, some regard a Holmes performance as a preview. They expect to travel; they want to know the choice sights for their future three-month jaunt to Ecuador. Some few, who consider themselves travel authorities, come to a Holmes lecture to point out gleefully the good things that he missed. "It makes them happy," Holmes says cheerfully. Tomorrow's audience, for the most, will be the same as the one that heard the Master exactly a year before. Generations of audiences inherit Holmes, one from the other.

An average Holmes lecture combines the atmosphere of a revival meeting and a family get-together at which home movies are shown. A typical Holmes travelogue begins in a brightly lit auditorium, at precisely three minutes after eight-thirty. The three minutes is to allow for latecomers. Holmes, attired in formal evening clothes, strides from the wings to center stage. People applaud; some cheer. Everyone seems to know him and to know exactly what to expect. Holmes smiles broadly. He is compact, proper, handsome. His goatee dominates the scene. He has worn it every season, with the exception of one in 1895 (when, beardless, he somewhat resembled Paget's Sherlock Holmes). Now, he speaks crisply. He announces that this is the third lecture of his fifty-fourth season. He announces his subject—"Adventures in Mexico."

He walks to one side of the stage, where a microphone is standing. The lights are dimmed. The auditorium becomes dark. Beyond the fifth row, Holmes cannot be seen. The all-color 16-mm film is projected on the screen. The film opens, minus title and credits, with a shot through the windshield of an automobile speeding down the Pan-American Highway to Monterrey. Holmes himself is the sound track. His speech, with just the hint of a theatrical accent, is intimate, as if he were talking in a living room. He punctuates descriptive passages with little formal jokes. When flowers and orange trees of Mexico are on the screen, he says, "We have movies and talkies, but now we should have smellies and tasties"—and he chuckles.

The film that he verbally captions is a dazzling, uncritical montage of Things Mexican. There is a señora selling tortillas, and close-ups of how tortillas are made. There is a bullfight, but not the kill. There is snow-capped Popocatepetl, now for sale at the bargain price of fifteen million dollars. There are the pyramids outside Mexico City, older than those of Egypt, built by the ancient Toltecs who went to war with wooden swords so that they would not kill their enemies.

Holmes's movies and lectures last two hours, with one intermission. The emphasis is on description, information, and oddity. Two potential ingredients are studiously omitted. One is adventure, the other politics. Holmes is never spectacular. "I want nothing dangerous. I don't care to emulate the explorers, to risk my neck, to be the only one or the first one there. Let others tackle the Himalayas, the Amazon, the North Pole, let them break the trails for me. I'm just a Cook's tourist, a little ahead of the crowd, but not too far ahead." Some years ago, Holmes did think that he was an explorer, and became very excited about it, he now admits sheepishly. This occurred in a trackless sector of Northern Rhodesia. Holmes felt that he had discovered a site never before seen by an outsider. Grandly, he planted the flag of the Explorers

Club, carefully he set up his camera, and then, as he prepared to shoot, his glance fell upon an object several feet away—an empty Kodak carton. Quietly, he repacked and stole away—and has stayed firmly on the beaten paths ever since.

As to politics, it never taints his lectures. He insists neither he nor his audiences are interested. "When you discuss politics," he says, "you are sure to offend." Even after his third trip to Russia, he refused to discuss politics. "I am a traveler," he explained at that time, "and not a student of political and economic questions. To me, Communism is merely one of the sights I went to see."

However, friends know that Holmes has his pet panacea for the ills of the world. He is violent about the gold standard, insisting that it alone can make all the world prosperous. Occasionally, when the mood is on him, and against his better judgment, he will inject propaganda in favor of the gold standard into an otherwise timid travelogue.

When he is feeling mellow, Holmes will confess that once in the past he permitted politics to intrude upon his sterile chitchat. It was two decades ago, when he jousted with Prohibition. While not a dedicated drinking man, Holmes has been on a friendly basis with firewater since the age of sixteen. In the ensuing years, he has regularly, every dusk before dinner, mixed himself one or two highballs. Only once did he try more than two, and the results were disastrous. "Any man who drinks three will drink three hundred," he now says righteously. Holmes felt that Prohibition was an insult to civilized living. As a consequence of this belief, his audiences during the days of the Eighteenth Amendment were often startled to hear Holmes extol the virtues of open drinking, in the middle of a placid discourse on Oberammergau or Lapland. "Sometimes an indignant female would return her tickets to the rest of my series," he says, "but there were others, more intelligent, to take her place."

This independent attitude in Holmes was solely the product of his personal success. Born in January, 1870, of a financially secure, completely cosmopolitan Chicago family, he was able to be independent from his earliest days. His father, an employee in the Third National Bank, distinguished himself largely by lending George Pullman enough cash to transform his old day coaches into the first Pullman Palace Sleeping Cars, and by refusing a half interest in the business in exchange for his help. Even to this day, it makes Burton Holmes dizzy to think of the money he might have saved in charges for Pullman berths.

Holmes's interest in show business began at the age of nine when his grandmother, Ann W. Burton, took him to hear John L. Stoddard lecture on the Passion Play at Oberammergau. Young Holmes was never the same again. After brief visits to faraway Florida and California, he quit school and accompanied his grandmother on his first trip abroad. He was sixteen and wide-eyed. His grandmother, who had traveled with her wine-salesman husband to France and Egypt and down the Volga in the sixties, was the perfect guide. But this journey through Europe was eclipsed, four years later, by a more important pilgrimage with his grandmother to Germany. The first day at his hotel in Munich, Holmes saw John L. Stoddard pass through the lobby reading a Baedeker. He was petrified. It was as if he had seen his Maker. Even now, over a half century later, when Holmes speaks about Stoddard, his voice carries a tinge of awe. For eighteen years of the later nineteenth century, Stoddard, with black-and-white slides and magnificent oratory, dominated the travel-lecture field. To audiences, young and old, he was the most romantic figure in America. Later, at Oberammergau, Holmes sat next to Stoddard through the fifteen acts of the Passion Play and they became friends.

When Holmes returned to the States, some months after Nellie Bly had made her own triumphal return to Brooklyn, he showed rare Kodak negatives of his travels to fellow members of the Chicago Camera Club. The members were impressed, and one suggested that these be mounted as slides and shown to the general public. "To take the edge off the silence, to keep the show moving," says Holmes, "I wrote an account of my journey and read it, as the stereopticon man changed slides." The show, which grossed the club $350, was Holmes's initial travelogue. However, he dates the beginning of his professional career from three years later, when he appeared under his own auspices with hand-colored slides.

After the Camera Club debut, Holmes did not go immediately into the travelogue field. He was not yet ready to appreciate its possibilities. Instead, he attempted to sell real estate, and failed. Then he worked for eight dollars a week as a photo supply clerk. In 1902, aching with wanderlust, he bullied his family into staking him to a five-month tour of Japan. On the boat he was thrilled to find John L. Stoddard, also bound for Japan. They became closer friends, even though they saw Nippon through different eyes. "The older man found Japan queer, quaint, comfortless, and almost repellent," Stoddard's son wrote years later. "To the younger man it was a fairyland." Stoddard invited Holmes to continue on around the world with him, but Holmes loved Japan and decided to remain.

When Holmes returned to Chicago, the World's Columbian Exposition of 1893 was in full swing. He spent months at the Jackson Park grounds, under Edison's new electric lights, listening to Lillian Russell sing, Susan B. Anthony speak, and watching Sandow perform feats of strength. With rising excitement, he observed Jim Brady eating, Anthony Comstock snorting at Little Egypt's hootchy-kootchy, and Alexander Dowie announcing himself as the Prophet Elijah III.

In the midst of this excitement came the depression of that year. Holmes's father suffered. "He hit the wheat pit at the wrong time, and I had to go out on my own," says Holmes. "The photo supply house offered me fifteen dollars a week to return. But I didn't want to work. The trip to Japan, the Oriental exhibits of the Exposition, were still on my mind. I thought of

Stoddard. I thought of the slides I'd had hand-colored in Tokyo. That was it, and it wasn't work. So I hired a hall and became a travel lecturer."

Copying society addresses from his mother's visiting list, and additional addresses from *The Blue Book,* Holmes mailed two thousand invitations in the form of Japanese poem-cards. Recipients were invited to two illustrated lectures, at $1.50 each, on "Japan—the Country and the Cities." Both performances were sellouts. Holmes grossed $700.

For four years Holmes continued his fight to win a steady following, but with only erratic success. Then, in 1897, when he stood at the brink of defeat, two events occurred to change his life. First, John L. Stoddard retired from the travel-lecture field and threw the platforms of the nation open to a successor. Second, Holmes supplemented colored slides with a new method of illustrating his talks. As his circular announced, "There will be presented for the first time in connection with a course of travel lectures a series of pictures to which a modern miracle has added the illusion of life itself—the reproduction of recorded motion."

Armed with his jumpy movies—scenes of the Omaha fire department, a police parade in Chicago, Italians eating spaghetti, each reel running twenty-five seconds, with a four-minute wait between reels—Burton Holmes invaded the Stoddard strongholds in the East. Stoddard came to hear him and observe the newfangled movies. Like Marshal Foch who regarded the airplane as "an impractical toy," Stoddard saw no future in the motion picture. Nevertheless, he gave young Holmes a hand by insisting that Augustin Daly lease his Manhattan theater to the newcomer. This done, Stoddard retired to the Austrian Tyrol, and Holmes went on to absorb Stoddard's audiences in Boston and Philadelphia and to win new followers of his own throughout the nation.

His success assured, Holmes began to gather material with a vigor that was to make him one of history's most indefatigable travelers. In 1900, at the Paris Exposition, sitting in a restaurant built like a Russian train, drinking vodka while a colored panorama of Siberia rolled past his window, he succumbed to this unique advertising of the new Trans-Siberian railway and bought a ticket. The trip in 1901 was a nightmare. After ten days on the Trans-Siberian train, which banged along at eleven miles an hour, Holmes was dumped into a construction train for five days, and then spent twenty-seven days on steamers going down the Amur River. It took him forty-two and a half days to travel from Moscow to Vladivostok.

But during that tour, he had one great moment. He saw Count Leo Tolstoi at Yasnaya Polyana, the author's country estate near Tula. At a dinner in Moscow, Holmes met Albert J. Beveridge, the handsome senator from Indiana. Beveridge had a letter of introduction to Tolstoi and invited Holmes and his enormous 60-mm movie camera to come along. Arriving in a four-horse landau, the Americans were surprised to find Tolstoi's house dilapidated. Then, they were kept waiting two hours. At last, the seventy-three-year-old, white-bearded Tolstoi, nine years away from his lonely death in a railway depot, appeared. He was attired in a mujik costume. He invited his visitors to breakfast, then conversed in fluent English. "He had only a slight accent, and he spoke with the cadence of Sir Henry Irving," Holmes recalls.

Of the entire morning's conversation, Holmes remembers clearly only one remark. That was when Tolstoi harangued, "There should be no law. No man should have the right to judge or condemn another. Absolute freedom of the individual is the only thing that can redeem the world. Christ was a great teacher, nothing more!" As Tolstoi continued to speak, Holmes quietly set up his movie camera. Tolstoi had never seen one before. He posed stiffly, as for a daguerreotype. When he thought that it was over, and resumed his talking, Holmes began actual shooting. This priceless film never reached the screen. Senator Beveridge was then a presidential possibility. His managers feared that this film of Beveridge with a Russian radical might be used by his opponents. The film was taken from Holmes and destroyed. Later, when he was not even nominated for the presidency, Beveridge wrote an apology to Holmes, "for this destruction of so valuable a living record of the grand old Russian."

In 1934, at a cost of ten dollars a day, Holmes spent twenty-one days in modern Soviet Russia. He loved the ballet, the omelets, the Russian rule against tipping, and the lack of holdups. He went twice to see the embalmed Lenin, fascinated by the sight of "his head resting on a red pillow like that of a tired man asleep."

Although Holmes's name had already appeared on eighteen travel volumes, this last Russian trip inspired him to write his first and only original book. The earlier eighteen volumes, all heavily illustrated, were offered as a set, of which over forty thousand were sold. However, they were not "written," but were actually a collection of lectures delivered orally by Holmes. The one book that he wrote as a book, *The Traveler's Russia,* published in 1934 by G.P. Putnam's Sons, was a failure. Holmes has bought the remainders and passes them out to guests with a variety of inscriptions. In a serious mood he will inscribe, "To travel is to possess the world." In a frivolous mood, he will write "With love from Tovarich Burtonovich Holmeski."

In the five decades past, Holmes has kept himself occupied with a wide variety of pleasures, such as attending Queen Victoria's Golden Jubilee in London, chatting with Admiral Dewey in Hong Kong, driving the first automobile seen in Denmark, and photographing a mighty eruption of Vesuvius.

In 1918, wearing a war correspondent's uniform, he shot army scenes on the Western Front and his films surpassed those of the poorly organized newsreel cameramen. In 1923, flying for the first time, he had his most dangerous experience, when his plane almost crashed between Toulouse and Rabat. Later, in

Berlin, he found his dollar worth ten million marks, and in Africa he interviewed Emperor Haile Selassie in French, and, closer to home, he flew 20,000 miles over Central and South America.

Burton Holmes enjoys company on his trips. By coincidence, they are often celebrities. Holmes traveled through Austria with Maria Jeritza, through Greece with E.F. Benson, through the Philippines with Dr. Victor Heiser. He covered World War I with Harry Franck, wandered about Japan with Lafcadio Hearn's son, crossed Ethiopia with the Duke of Gloucester. He saw Hollywood with Mary Pickford, Red Square with Alma Gluck, and the Andes with John McCutcheon.

Of the hundreds of travelogues that Holmes has delivered, the most popular was "The Panama Canal." He offered this in 1912, when the "big ditch" was under construction, and news-hungry citizens flocked to hear him. Among less timely subjects, his most popular was the standard masterpiece on Oberammergau, followed closely by his illustrated lectures on the "Frivolities of Paris," the "Canals of Venice," the "Countryside of England" and, more currently, "Adventures in Mexico." Burton Holmes admits that his greatest failure was an elaborate travelogue on Siam, even though it seemed to have everything except Anna and the King thereof. Other failures included travelogues on India, Burma, Ethiopia, and—curiously—exotic Bali. The only two domestic subjects to fizzle were "Down in Dixie" in 1915 and "The Century of Progress Exposition" in 1932.

All in all, the success of Holmes's subjects has been so consistently high that he has never suffered seriously from competition. One rival died, another retired eight years ago. "I'm the lone survivor of the magic-lantern boys," says Holmes. Of the younger crowd, Holmes thought that Richard Halliburton might become his successor. "He deserved to carry the banner," says Holmes. "He was good-looking, with a fine classical background, intelligent, interesting, and he really did those darn-fool stunts." Halliburton, who had climbed the Matterhorn, swum the Hellespont, followed the Cortés train through Mexico, lectured with slides. "I told him to throw away the slides," says Holmes. "He was better without them, his speech was so colorful." When Halliburton died attempting to sail a Chinese junk across the Pacific, Holmes decided to present an illustrated lecture on "The Romantic Adventures of Richard Halliburton." He used his own movies but, in the accompanying talk, Halliburton's written text. "It was a crashing failure," sighs Holmes. "His millions of fans did not want to hear me, and my fans did not want to know about him."

For a while, Hollywood appeared to be the travelogue's greatest threat. Holmes defeated this menace by marriage with the studios. He signed a contract with Paramount, made fifty-two travel shorts each year, between 1915 and 1921. Then, with the advent of talking pictures, Holmes joined Metro-Goldwyn-Mayer and made a series of travelogues, released in English, French, Italian, Spanish. In 1933, he made his debut in radio, and in 1944 made his first appearance on television.

Today, safe in the knowledge that he is an institution, Holmes spends more and more time in his rambling, plantation-style, wooden home, called "Topside," located on a hill a mile above crowded Hollywood Boulevard. This dozen-roomed brown house, once a riding club for silent day film stars, and owned for six years by Francis X. Bushman (who gave it Hollywood's first swimming pool, where Holmes now permits neighborhood children to splash), was purchased by Holmes in 1930. "I had that M-G-M contract," he says, "and it earned me a couple of hundred thousand dollars. Well, everyone with a studio contract immediately gets himself a big car, a big house, and a small blonde. I acquired the car, the house, but kept the blonde a mental acquisition." For years, Holmes also owned a Manhattan duplex decorated with costly Japanese and Buddhist treasures, which he called "Nirvana." Before Pearl Harbor, Holmes sold the duplex, with its two-million-dollar collection of furnishings, to Robert Ripley, the cartoonist and oddity hunter.

Now, in his rare moments of leisure, Holmes likes to sit on the veranda of his Hollywood home and chat with his wife. Before he met her, he had been involved in one public romance. Gossips, everywhere, insisted that he might marry the fabulous Elsie de Wolfe, actress, millionaire decorator, friend of Oscar Wilde and Sarah Bernhardt, who later became Lady Mendl. Once, in Denver, Holmes recalls, a reporter asked him if he was engaged to Elsie de Wolfe. Holmes replied, curtly, No. That afternoon a banner headline proclaimed: BURTON HOLMES REFUSES TO MARRY ELSIE DE WOLFE!

Shortly afterward, during a photographic excursion, Holmes met Margaret Oliver who, suffering from deafness, had taken up still photography as an avocation. In 1914, following a moonlight proposal on a steamer's deck, he married Miss Oliver in New York City's St. Stephen's Episcopal Church, and took her to prosaic Atlantic City for the first few days of their honeymoon, then immediately embarked on a long trip abroad.

When his wife is out shopping, Holmes will stroll about his estate, study his fifty-four towering palm trees, return to the veranda for a highball, thumb through the *National Geographic,* play with his cats, or pick up a language textbook. He is on speaking terms with eight languages, including some of the Scandinavian, and is eager to learn more. He never reads travel books. "As Pierre Loti once remarked, 'I don't read. It might ruin my style,'" he explains.

He likes visitors, and he will startle them with allusions to his earlier contemporaries. "This lawn part reminds me of the one at which I met Emperor Meiji," he will say. Meiji, grandfather of Hirohito, opened Japan to Commodore Perry. When visitors ask for his travel advice, Holmes invariably tells them to see the Americas first. "Why go to Mont St. Michel?" he asks. "Have you seen Monticello?"

But when alone with his wife and co-workers on the veranda,

and the pressure of the new season is weeks away, he will loosen his blue dressing gown, inhale, then stare reflectively out over the sun-bathed city below.

"You know, this is the best," he will say softly, "looking down on this Los Angeles. It is heaven. I could sit here the rest of my life." Then, suddenly, he will add, "There is so much else to see and do. If only I could have another threescore years upon this planet. If only I could know the good earth better than I do."

———————

Note: Irving Wallace (1916-1990) wrote this article on the occasion of Burton Holmes's 77th birthday. It was originally printed in *The Saturday Evening Post* May 10, 1947. Holmes retired the following year from presenting his travelogues in person. He died in 1958 at age 88. His autobiography, *The World is Mine,* was published in 1953.

Reprinted by permission of Mrs. Sylvia Wallace.

BURTON HOLMES

By Arthur M. Schlesinger, jr.

B urton Holmes!—forgotten today, but such a familiar name in America in the first half of the 20th century, a name then almost synonymous with dreams of foreign travel. In the era before television brought the big world into the households of America, it was Burton Holmes who brought the world to millions of Americans in crowded lecture halls, and did so indefatigably for 60 years. I still remember going with my mother in the 1920s to Symphony Hall in Boston, watching the brisk, compact man with a Vandyke beard show his films of Venice or Bali or Kyoto and describe foreign lands in engaging and affectionate commentary.

Burton Holmes invented the word "travelogue" in 1904. He embodied it for the rest of his life. He was born in Chicago in 1870 and made his first trip abroad at the age of 16. Taking a camera along on his second trip, he mounted his black-and-white negatives on slides and showed them to friends in the Chicago Camera Club. "To keep the show moving," he said later, "I wrote an account of my journey and read it, as the stereopticon man changed slides." He had discovered his métier. Soon he had his slides hand-colored and was in business as a professional lecturer. In time, as technology developed, slides gave way to moving pictures.

Holmes was a tireless traveler, forever ebullient and optimistic, uninterested in politics and poverty and the darker side of life, in love with beautiful scenery, historic monuments, picturesque customs, and challenging trips. He was there at the Athens Olympics in 1896, at the opening of the Trans-Siberian railway, at the Passion Play in Oberammergau. His popular lectures had such titles as "The Magic of Mexico," "The Canals of Venice," "The Glories and Frivolities of Paris." His illustrated travel books enthralled thousands of American families. He also filmed a series of travelogues—silent pictures for Paramount, talkies for Metro-Goldwyn-Mayer.

He wanted his fellow countrymen to rejoice in the wonders of the great globe. "I'm a Cook's tourist," he said, referring to the famous tours conducted by Thomas Cook and Sons, "reporting how pleasant it is in such and such a place." He knew that the world was less than perfect, but he thought the worst sufficiently documented, and his mission, as he saw it, was to bring people the best. Reflecting at the end of the Second World War on the mood of returning veterans, he said, "The atrocities and miseries will be difficult to forget. I know I can't give my Beautiful Italy lecture next session to men who know Italy only as a pigsty . . . One day these boys will forget and come to my lectures not to hoot but to relive the better moments and enjoy themselves."

When he retired in 1951, Burton Holmes had delivered over 8,000 lectures. By the time he died in 1958, television had taken over the job he had discharged so ardently for more than half a century. He taught generations of Americans about the great world beyond the seas. His books are still readable today and show new generations how their grandparents learned about a world that has since passed away but remains a fragrant memory.

THE WORLD 100 YEARS AGO

By Dr. Fred Israel

The generation that lived 100 years ago was the first to leave behind a comprehensive visual record. It was the camera that made this possible. The great photographers of the 1860s and 1870s took their unwieldy equipment to once-unimaginable places—from the backstreets of London to the homesteads of the American frontier; from tribal Africa to the temples of Japan. They photographed almost the entire world.

Burton Holmes (1870-1958) ranks among the pioneers who popularized photojournalism. He had an insatiable curiosity. "There was for me the fascination of magic in photography," Holmes wrote. "The word Kodak had not yet been coined. You could not press the button and let someone else do the rest. You had to do it all yourself and know what you were doing." Holmes combined his love of photography with a passion for travel. It didn't really matter where—only that it be exciting.

"Shut your eyes, tight!" said Holmes. "Imagine the sands of the Sahara, the temples of Japan, the beach at Waikiki, the fjords of Norway, the vastness of Panama, the great gates of Peking." It was this type of visual imagination that made Burton Holmes America's best known travel lecturer. By his 75th birthday, he had crossed the Atlantic Ocean 30 times and the Pacific 20, and he had gone around the world on six occasions. Variety magazine estimated that in his five-decade career, Holmes had delivered more than 8,000 lectures describing almost every corner of the earth.

Burton Holmes was born in Chicago on January 8, 1870. His privileged background contributed to his lifelong fascination with travel. When he was 16, his maternal grandmother took him on a three-month European trip, about which he later wrote:

> I still recall our first meal ashore, the delicious English sole served at the Adelphi Hotel [Liverpool] . . . Edinburgh thrilled me, but Paris! I would gladly have travelled third class or on a bike or on foot. Paris at last! I knew my Paris in advance. Had I not studied the maps and plans? I knew I could find my way to Notre Dame and to the Invalides without asking anyone which way to go. (The Eiffel Tower had not yet been built.) From a bus-top, I surveyed the boulevards—recognizing all the famous sights. Then for a panoramic survey of the city, I climbed the towers of Notre Dame, then the Tour St. Jacques, the Bastille Column, and finally the Arc De Triomphe, all in one long day. That evening, I was in Montmartre, where as yet there stood no great domed church of the Sacre Coeur. But at the base of the famous hill were the red windmill wings of the Moulin Rouge revolving in all their majesty. My French—school French—was pretty bad but it sufficed. Paris was the springtime of my life!

Holmes never lost his passion for travel nor his passion for capturing his observations on film. He has left us with a unique and remarkable record that helps us to visualize the world many decades ago.

Lecturing became Holmes's profession. In 1892-93 he toured Japan. He discovered that "it was my native land in some previous incarnation—and the most beautiful land I have known." Holmes had the idea of giving an illustrated lecture about Japan to an affluent Chicago audience:

> I had brought home a large number of Japanese cards such as
> are used in Japan for sending poems or New Year's greetings.
> They were about two inches by fourteen inches long. I had the
> idea that they would, by their odd shape, attract instant notice.
> So I had envelopes made for them, employing a Japanese artist
> to make a design.

Holmes sent about 2,000 invitations to the socially prominent
whose addresses he took from the *Blue Book*. He "invited" them
to two illustrated lectures at $1.50 each on "Japan—the Country
and the Cities." ($1.50 was a high sum for the 1890s considering
that the average worker earned about $1 per day.) Both perfor-
mances sold out.

Burton Holmes's "Travelogues" (he began using the term in
1904) rapidly became part of American upper class societal life.
Holmes engaged the best theater or concert hall for a week at a
time. His appearance was an annual event at Carnegie Hall in
New York, Symphony Hall in Boston, and Orchestra Hall in
Chicago. His uncanny instinct for exciting programs invariably
received rave reviews. Once he explained how he selected his
photographic subjects:

> If I am walking through Brussels and see a dog cart or some
> other unimportant thing that is interesting enough for me to
> watch it, I am totally certain others would be interested in seeing
> a photograph of it.

A conservative man, Holmes avoided political upheavals,
economic exploitation, and social conflicts in his travelogues.
"When you discuss politics," he said, "you are sure to offend."
Holmes focused on people, places, and customs. He offered his
audience a world which was unfailingly tranquil and beautiful.

In 1897, Holmes introduced motion picture segments into his
programs. ("Neapolitans Eating Spaghetti" was his first film
clip.) His engaging personality contributed to his success. His

crisp narrative was delivered in a pleasant and cultured tone. He always wore formal dress with striped pants before an audience. Holmes took pride in creating an atmosphere so that his listeners could imagine the "Magic of Mexico" or the "Frivolities of Paris." "My first ambition was to be a magician," he said. "And, I never departed from creating illusions. I have tried to create the illusion that we are going on a journey. By projecting the views, I tried to create the illusion we are looking through 'the window of travel' upon shifting scenes." Holmes's travelogues were immensely successful financially—and Holmes became one of history's most indefatigable travelers.

Holmes's lectures took place during the winter months between the 1890s and his retirement in the early 1950s. In between, he traveled—he crossed Morocco on horseback from oasis to oasis (1894); he was in the Philippines during the 1899 insurrection; in 1901, he traversed the Russian Empire, going from Moscow to Vladivostok in 43 days. He visited Yellowstone National Park (1896) before it had been fully mapped. He was always on the move, traveling to: Venice (1896); London (1897); Hawaii (1898); The Philippines (1899); Paris (1900); Russia, China, and Korea (1901-02); Madeira, Lisbon, Denmark, and Sweden (1902); Arizona, California, and Alaska (1903); Switzerland (1904); Russia and Japan (1905); Italy, Greece, Egypt, and Hong Kong (1906); Paris, Vienna, and Germany (1907); Japan (1908); Norway (1909); Germany and Austria (1910); Brazil, Argentina, and Peru (1911); Havana and Panama (1912); India and Burma (1913); the British Isles (1914); San Francisco (1915); Canada (1916); Australia and New Zealand (1917); Belgium and Germany (1919); Turkey and the Near East (1920); England (1921); China (1922); North Africa (1923); Italy (1924); Ceylon (1925); Holland (1926); France (1927); Spain (1928); London (1929); Ethiopia (1930); California (1931); Java (1932); Chicago (1933); the Soviet Union (1934); Normandy and Brittany (1935); South America (1936); South Africa (1937); Germany (1938).

Holmes's black and white photographs have extraordinary clarity. His sharp eye for the unusual ranks him as a truly outstanding photographer and chronicler of the world.

Holmes's lectures on the Panama Canal were his most popular—cities added extra sessions. For Holmes though, his favorite presentation was always Paris—"no city charms and fascinates us like the city by the Seine." He found Athens in the morning to be the most beautiful scene in the world—"with its pearl lights and purple-blue shadows and the Acropolis rising in mystic grandeur." Above all though, Japan remained his favorite land—"one can peel away layer after layer of the serene contentment which we mistake for expressionlessness and find new beauties and surprises beneath each." And Kyoto, once the capital, was the place he wanted most to revisit—and revisit. Holmes never completed a travelogue of New York City—"I am saving the biggest thing in the world for the last." At the time of his death in 1958 at age 88, Holmes had visited most of the world. He repeatedly told interviewers that he had lived an exciting and fulfilling life because he had accomplished his goal—to travel.

In a time before television, Burton Holmes was for many people "The Travelogue Man." He brought the glamour and excitement of foreign lands to Americans unable to go themselves. His successful career spanned the years from the Spanish-American War in 1898 to the Cold War of the 1950s—a period when Americans were increasingly curious about distant places and peoples. During this time period, travel was confined to a comparative handful of the privileged. Holmes published travelogues explaining foreign cultures and customs to the masses.

In this series of splendid travel accounts, Holmes unfolds before our eyes the beauties of foreign lands as they appeared almost a century ago. These volumes contain hundreds of photographs taken by Holmes. Through his narratives and illustrations we are transported in spirit to the most interesting countries and cities of the world.

Moscow

In 1898, in Russia, a small meeting of workers' delegates formed what would become the Communist Party of the Soviet Union. For the next 19 years, Vladimir Lenin and his followers planned, worked, and fought to overthrow Czar Nicholas II.

In 1904-5, Japan humiliated Russian military forces in every battle of the Russo-Japanese War. Bad news from the front fueled criticism of Nicholas's autocratic government. Student protests increased and workers went on strike. Lenin printed a newspaper in Geneva that was smuggled into Russia. Sailors on the battleship *Potemkin* in the Black Sea threw their officers overboard and turned their heavy guns on towns along the shore. Assassinations by terrorists increased. Advocates of land reform adopted a new, stronger, slogan: All Land to the Peasants.

Burton Holmes's account of Moscow is devoid of politics. He came to see what the city had to show. For those "who ask for history and statistics," he advised his readers, "there are ponderous tomes in every library." Holmes visited Moscow in 1901. His written and photographic description of the people, their traditions, and their customs is a wonderful primary source for understanding everyday life in the capital city of the Russian Empire.

He visited Count Leo Tolstoi, then 72. Photographs of Tolstoi and his family are included in this volume. He toured the vast Simonoff Monastery, describing "fanatical peasant women" following a Madonna icon. At another monastery, he was fascinated by "a mob of peasants fighting for a chance to pay for the privilege of kissing the frontal bone of some defunct old worthy laid out in a silver coffin."

Holmes focused on everyday life in Moscow, a city of more than one million people. He took more than 700 photographs—152 are included in this book. He described the neighborhoods, the hospitals, the public baths, the hotels, the theaters, and the restaurants, as well as the markets and shops.

The reader can perceive the vast gap between the rich and the poor and the strong influence of religion in everyday life, although this was not Holmes's intention in this brilliant study of the people of Moscow in 1901. Sixteen years after his visit, class revolution would convulse Russia; this revolution would profoundly affect the course of 20th-century history.

INTERIOR OF THE CHURCH OF THE HOLY SAVIOR

OSCOW

MOSCOW is in every sense the metropolis of Russia.
While the site of St. Petersburg was only an expanse
of barren marshes, the Imperial ancestors of Peter dwelt in
palaces of stone upon the Kremlin Hill.

Moscow is even older than the Empire. She is indeed
the mother city of the Russians. The history of Moscow
until the founding of St. Petersburg is the history of Russia.
The old and the new capitals are strikingly dissimilar. St.
Petersburg, with a population of one million three hundred

thousand, is an artificial product, forced into being by the imperious will of one astounding man,—the man whose name it bears, Peter the Great.

Moscow, which has to-day a population of nearly one million, is the natural outgrowth of a mighty people : the center toward which the Slavonic race has always looked for inspiration, in politics and in religion : the stronghold whence the early Tsars of Muscovy reached out for the dominion of the Slavonic world. St. Petersburg is European ; Moscow is Muscovite. Petersburg stands stiffly on the flat islands of the Neva, rigid in her assumed, imported architectural garb of Roman arches and Grecian façades.

Moscow sits gracefully in the fair valley of the Moskva, robed in the green of gardens, wearing with pride and distinction her semi-oriental splendors, crowned with a diadem of blue and golden domes. St. Petersburg impresses — Moscow fascinates, the traveler. From St. Petersburg to

THE MOSCOW GATE, ST. PETERSBURG

Moscow the distance is about four hundred miles, as the crow flies. Our train will emulate the crow, for the railway runs in a bee-line to the old capital. It is a most significant illustration of autocratic power, this railway-line that turns aside for no natural barrier, that does not swerve from its

THE KREMLIN AND THE MOSKVA

straight course for any reason urged by expediency or the demands of Russian commerce or Russian industries. The railway shuns the towns and the factories; it traverses a marshy desert; it touches only one place of importance, and that one merely because it lies directly in its path. Why was it so constructed? Because the Tsar, Nicholas I, thus willed it. Several routes had been outlined by his ministers. The Tsar, rightly suspecting interested motives on the part of the champions of every scheme, by a bold action placed himself in the category with Solomon, Alexander, and Columbus. He laid a ruler on the map and drew a straight line from the new to the old capital, saying, "You will build the railway thus." Hence, to-day, the traveler speeds over four hundred

A COURIER TRAIN

miles of track, straight and unerring as the judgment of
the Tsar, without a single political curve, or a single side-
track leading into private pockets.   Would that we had an
honest Tsar presiding over every city council in our land!
We complete the fourteen-hour journey during the night in a
"Courier Train," approaching Moscow in the morning at
what the Russians call high speed.

THE RAILWAY STATION

THE VLADIMIR GATE

From the first moment, Moscow impresses us as being unlike any other city in the world. To be unique is the chief charm of a city, and undoubtedly Moscow is unique. Within ten minutes after our arrival we have seen a hundred

THE ILINSKAYA GATE

A BOULEVARD

curious things that we have never seen before. Details appeal to me perhaps too strongly to insure a proper balance in summing up impressions of travel; still, I maintain that the illusion of reality' in our photographic journeys can be most vividly produced by dwelling on the little things that may appear at first altogether too trivial and insignificant to mention. Frankly, I did not come to study Moscow, I came to *see* what Moscow had to show, and to enjoy such new

A PROMENADE

sensations as she would vouchsafe me. For those who ask for history and statistics, there are ponderous tomes in every library where the deeds of Moscow's makers and the volume of her commerce are set down in full. We for the moment are more interested in the picturesque peculiarities of everyday street-life and in the novel aspect of all things Muscovite. All that we see delights us, because it is all Russian. The walls, the gates, the towers, and the chapels, the blue and golden domes that we have read about, are here — but they are

THE SOUKAREFF TOWER

even more picturesque and richer in color than we had dared to hope. Of course, this pictorial quaintness and brilliancy

FROM THE SOUKAREFF TOWER

HATTERS

cannot go on *crescendo* throughout the entire period of our experiences in Moscow. In a city of a million people there must be long avenues of commonplaceness, interminable stretches of monotony, paved (as we soon discover) with

the cruelest cobblestones that have ever racked a carriage. The houses in the residential quarters are not high; two stories is the rule, three the exception, and four almost extraordinary. In a great many of the broader boulevards, trees are ranged in quadruple rows, bordering a central promenade which

TAILORS

BOLCHAYA MOSKOVSKAYA GASTINITSA

is almost entirely shut off from the traffic of the noisy street upon both sides by screens of verdure.

But everywhere, like the dominant notes of a sacred symphony, we see the little golden domes fixed on the blue page of the sky,—the expression of a harmonic chord written by the hand of faith above this most religious and devout of Russian cities.   Over Moscow, domes, like the stars of old,

THE HISTORICAL MUSEUM

seem to sing together in the heavens.   Some are green —
like the trees and the roofs of Moscow ; some are blue — like
the skies and the eyes of the Russians ; but most are gold —
like the treasures and icons of Orthodoxy that sleep in the
safe guardianship of the silent old churches.

An excellent point of vantage for a bird's-eye view of
Moscow is the summit of the Soukhareff Tower which was
built about 1690 by Peter the Great, and named in honor of
a regiment that had protected him, when, in his childhood,
the faction called the Strelitz rose against him.   It has been,
by turns, seat of the Council of State, Council Chamber of a
Masonic Lodge, Naval School, and College of Admiralty, and
it is now a water-tower, containing a vast reservoir.   Around

THE SLAVIANSKY BAZAR

DINING-HALL IN THE HOTEL DU BAZAR SLAVE

the tower surges on every Sunday morning a market where the mujiks come to buy hats and caps and various articles of clothing; but strange to say we do not see a single Jew in this commercial mob. There are a few Tatar merchants, with unpleasing faces and with a greasy, Oriental air about them that inclines us to favor the equally fragrant, but decidedly more healthy-looking Russians.

THE GRAND THEATER

A tableau formed by a hat-merchant and his customer reminds us that human nature is the same in all parts of the world. A similar tableau may be witnessed every day in the shops of Knox or Dunlap; the same insistent seller — the same embarrassed buyer — liking the new hat not half so well as the old one he is now discarding, and yet dreading not to buy for fear the salesman will think he does not know his own mind.

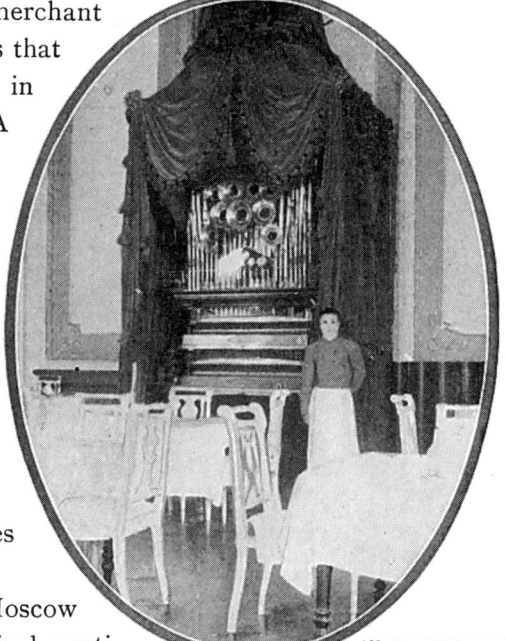

AN ORCHESTRION

The caravansaries of Moscow are of two kinds: the typical continental hotel, and the Russian Gastinitsa, of which the Bolchaya Moskovskaya Gastinitsa is the most magnificent. In every detail it is thoroughly Russian. The foreigner who can speak the language will find that the native Gastinitsa is far more attractive than the hy-

IN THE AQUARIUM GARDENS

brid hotels; but if
he speaks not the
Slavonic tongue,
he had better pa-
tronize the cele-
brated Slaviansky
Bazar, where the
servants have a
slight knowledge
of the continental
languages. On
entering the salle-

STAINED GLASS FROM AMERICA

à-manger of the Slaviansky Bazar — one of the most famous
in Russia — a traveler said, ''Why,'' ''I thought the Slaviansky Bazar was an old slave market!'' In reality it is
nothing but a big hotel,—a rambling bazar or gathering
place for the Slavs who come to see the mother city of the
Slavonic Empire. One feature of the Russian restaurants

THE RESTAURANT OF THE AQUARIUM

that strikes the ear is a gigantic automatic organ or orchestrion which heaves, blows, thumps, and bangs out old-fashioned bits from "Mignon," "Martha," and the "Mascotte."

The largest open space in Moscow is the Square of the Theaters, bounded on three sides by temples of the drama, of which the largest is one of the most splendid theaters in the world, having places for four thousand auditors. But as our visit comes in June, we find the theaters closed in favor of the summer gardens, which form a distinctive attraction in all Russian cities. At the Aquarium patrons have the

A GROCERY-STORE

THE SANDOUNOVSKAYA BATHS

choice of four different kinds of entertainment. Upon an open stage, troops of Russian peasants perform their wonderfully acrobatic dances, and sing their weird and elemental songs, strong, vigorous, national chants, ballads which sound to us refreshingly noble and poetic — a most blessed relief to American ears, which are so often offended in our popular resorts with that despicable musical perversion, appropriately known as "rag

IN A RUSSIAN BATH

A MODERN EDIFICE

time," so shameless and so cheap in its vivid suggestion
of vulgarity. May its vogue be brief!

Then there is a splendid restaurant, lighted like a cathedral with beautiful stained-glass, imported by the way from
the United States; not, however, of ecclesiastical design.
Dinners are served at a cost of from sixty-five cents to a
dollar and fifteen cents; but if you come after hours, the
prices *à la carte* are startlingly out of proportion, and, curiously enough, the regular dinner-hour is fixed at a time when

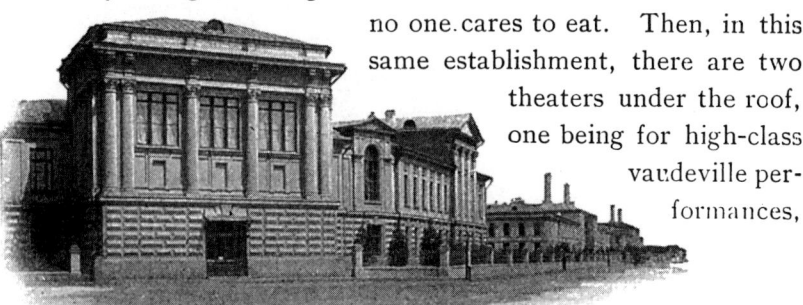

no one cares to eat. Then, in this
same establishment, there are two
theaters under the roof,
one being for high-class
vaudeville per-
formances,

CLINIC OF THE UNIVERSITY

THE TVERSKAYA

and the other for grand opera sung by the artists who in the winter season grace the boards of the Imperial opera-houses.

Moscow is usually regarded as a beautiful but backward, almost medieval, city. Let us correct this false impression with a few glimpses of her modern aspects. Even in such details as grocery-stores, Moscow is not behind New York, and is far ahead of Paris, as is proved by an illustration

OF THE MASSES

FÊTE POPULAIRE

showing the interior of a superb establishment situated in the Tverskaya. Russia is usually regarded as the home of the unwashed. Nowhere in all the world, save possibly in ancient Rome, have any nobler temples been erected to the admirable god of cleanliness. To-day the public baths of Moscow are the finest in the world. The famous Sandounov-skaya baths are housed in a palatial structure three stories high, cover-ing one city block, and entirely devoted to vari-ous kinds of baths, from the cheap " scrubbery " for mujiks, where common folk

A MOSCOW TRAM

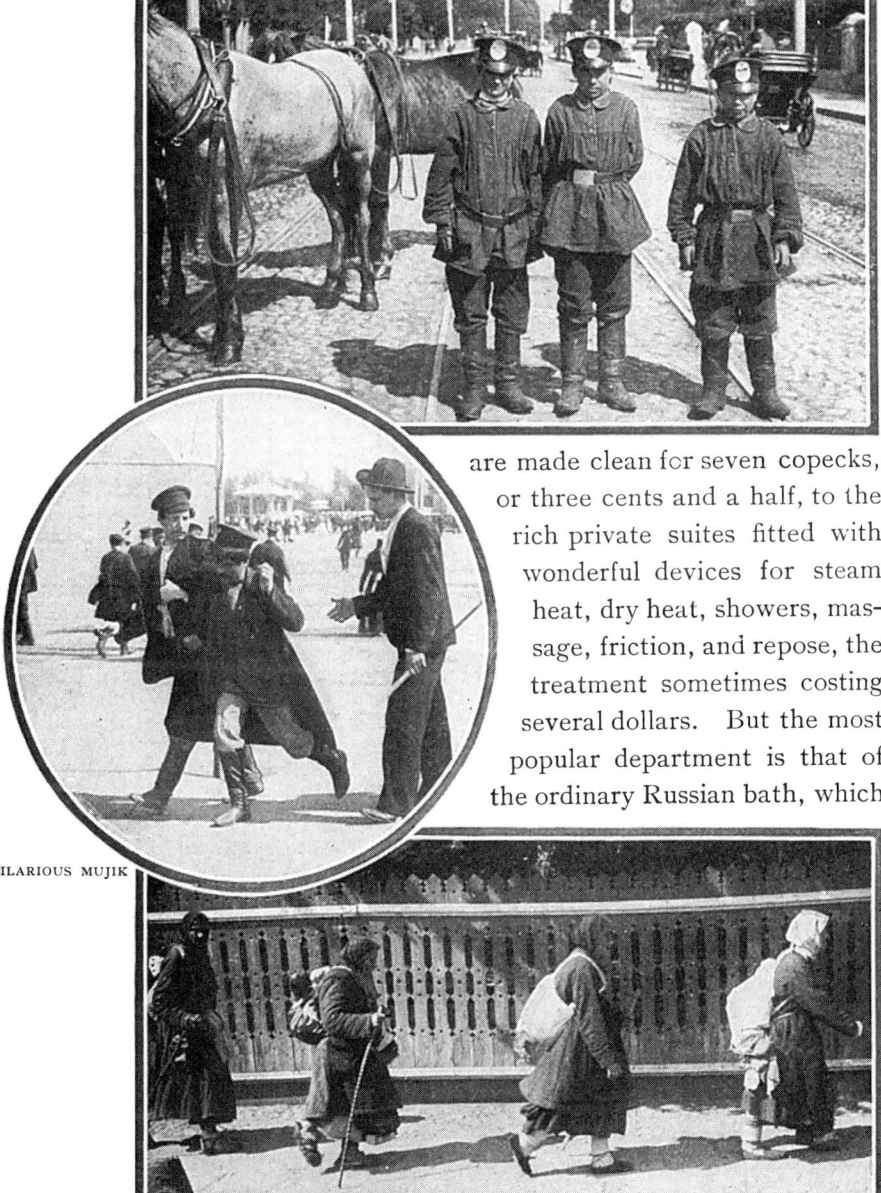

ILARIOUS MUJIK

are made clean for seven copecks, or three cents and a half, to the rich private suites fitted with wonderful devices for steam heat, dry heat, showers, massage, friction, and repose, the treatment sometimes costing several dollars. But the most popular department is that of the ordinary Russian bath, which

PEASANT WOMEN

costs about half a dollar, and is thronged
every afternoon by the business men
of Moscow. There we invariably
sought refreshment and reju-
venation at the close of our
long days of sightseeing and
photographic work. As for

THE OMNIPRESI
SAMOVAR

DEMOLITION

THE TERRACE AT THE SPARROW HILLS

public institutions, the new clinic of the university is one of the best equipped in Europe, with beds for six hundred patients, while the Foundling Asylum is the largest in the world, caring for 33,000 babies in the course of the year. It is supported by a tax on playing cards.

Russia is usually regarded as the home of semi-savages, glazed over with a veneer of polish, through which the bar-

FEASTING ON CAVIAR AND VISTAS

baric Tatar is instantly attainable by the finger-nails of those who dare to scratch the Russian. But nowhere in all the world have I found the police so unfailingly polite, or the people more considerate and courteous to the foreigner. I

PANORAMA FRO

do not speak without experience. I took seven hundred photographs in Moscow,—I had seven hundred interviews with policemen. Each one began with a salute, a courteous demand to see my permit-papers, or my "bou-maga"; then a careful perusal of the permits, an apology, and a farewell salute.

I did my best to get arrested, knowing that such a happy mishap would delight my managers at home, for it would result in much gratuitous publicity. I nearly succeeded on the day of a great popular fête. My permits to photograph in Moscow did not cover such occasions. The

VIRGINS OF THE SISTERHOOD

officer politely begged us to ask permission to make a motion-
picture of the scene from the commissaire.   Our guide goes
off in search of that official while we set up the instruments.
As he does not return, and as the crowd about us is increas-

THE SPARROW HILLS

ing, we turn on the machine, make
the picture, pack up and take
our places in our cab.   At
last the guide comes with the
answer of the commissaire,
who refuses our request,
saying that he fears that
we may create a tumult.
Therefore the picture of
the carrousel is only an
optical illusion for, offi-
cially, we never made it.
Then we mingle with the
happy crowds, quietly snap-
shooting right and left, but
apparently not attracting any

A MODERN TOMB

attention, until a big policeman informs me that he has orders
to take me into custody, unless I leave the grounds at once.
While meeting our protesting arguments with courtesy, he
cleverly edges us outside the limits of this recreation-ground,
and then, having performed the letter of his instructions,
refuses to arrest us.　　But he takes the number of the cab
and writes down the replies of the frightened driver, whom
he questions as to our lodging-place and nationality.

But I was not the only man led off the field that day.
No; there were several others who made inglorious exits
from the festive scene, as is confirmed by the picture of a
tipsy mujik, which reminds us of a popular slang-expression
so apt in this connection that I must beg leave to use the
term — it is "a joyful jag." Let those who disapprove and
refuse to comprehend the picturesque language written by
George Ade and Billy Baxter, and spoken by the Weber-
fieldians, look in their dictionaries, and they will find that
"jag" has two legitimate applications in this case ; for the
word "jag" is defined in the Century Dictionary both as a
"zigzag" and as "a lot, a load, or a quantity." The
mujik, when engaged in conveying his "lot, load, and

A CARROUSEL

quantity '' along his '' zigzag '' homeward way, is the most
hopelessly hilarious individual in the world.   The universe is
his, he loves it ; he worships every passer-by, even to the
point of fond embraces ; he sings and laughs and shouts and

MOSCOW SEEN FROM THE SPARROW HILLS

staggers in such a hearty, happy, and good-humored way that
we forgive him all his sins instanter, because he is so open-
hearted and so merry, without a single trace of the surliness
and brutality that immoderate indulgence in wine or beer
usually brings to the Anglo-Saxon toper.

But if vodka claims its usual toll of victims among the
working-classes, tea is the panacea of both rich and poor —
the samovar is the salvation of the thirsty Russians, and
counts its devotees by millions.   The Muscovite's conception
of perfect bliss includes a glass, a pot of tea, and the samovar
singing beside him in the wilderness.   The traveler learns to
love the samovar.   Its comforting omnipresence is one of the
joys of Russian travel ; hot water, strong delicious tea, may
be had at any time of day or night, and everywhere — in
trains, hotels, or in suburban woods, where the bright brass
machine may be rented for a few copecks a day.

The Russians are extremely fond of nature. On holidays the city folk flock to the woods at the base of what are called the Sparrow Hills — a height whence Moscow was first viewed in 1812 by Napoleon. A breezy restaurant is perched upon the crest, and there we may feast on caviar and vistas simultaneously. We observe with silent commendation the characteristic costume of the Russian waiter, the white blouse and trousers, spotless apron and red sash, decidedly better adapted to the needs of his vocation than the black, graceless, spotted, and unkempt dress-coat that airs its shabby gentility in the restaurants of other countries.

But we came here to enjoy the panorama. We were not disappointed, although a photograph must of necessity make Moscow microscopic from this point of view. One feature only stands out with appreciable relief — the vast square enceinte of a convent on the left. It is the Novo Devitchy Monastyr, or New Convent of the Virgins. Founded in 1524, the convent has known many royal inmates — one, a Tsarina who voluntarily cloistered herself within its walls ; one, the ambitious sister of Peter the Great, who was imprisoned there, and from her windows saw the execution of the Strelitz

NOVO DEVITCHY CONVENT

THE REFECTORY

leaders who had supported her presumptions to the throne.
The ensemble is strikingly beautiful in color and in form. It
is impossible to picture the intense red of the towers, impossible to lavish too much gilding on the domes. The gates

THE MIDDAY MEAL

are wide open and unguarded. We enter freely, finding ourselves in a broad open space with modern tombs upon one
side. Two of the black-robed virgins of the Sisterhood turn
their young faces toward the graves as we approach. We
wander into several churches, listen to the chanting of a

SIMONOFF MONASTERY

female choir, and then, as no one pays the slightest heed to
us, we push our investigations further to find ourselves in the
refectory. Then we are finally discovered by the Mother
Superior. She cordially insists that we shall stay to lunch-
eon with her flock of solemn little women, who presently file
in and take their places. One sister reads a lesson from the
book, the others perform miracles — that is, they eat the
awful food that is set down before them, and drink the revolting kvass, made from the crumbs of old, black, bitter bread.
We paid dearly for the picture of the refectory. We had to
eat of the same fare, and *we* were *not* used to it. Then, to
our horror, after we had succeeded in doing rebellious justice

to a revolting soup, the kind old mother, wishing to honor the strangers, sent with her compliments, two pewter plates brimming with a still more impossible concoction, which she had ordered especially for us. We base our claim to a place in the Orthodox Paradise upon the fact that we consumed that extra dose. Before departing we made an offering of several roubles, whereupon the ancient dame, lifting her hands in benison, exclaimed: '' The Americans are the only people who should be allowed to exist!'' The Simonoff Monastery upon the eastern outskirts of the city is one of the richest and most beautiful of the many monastic abodes that abound in and about Moscow. The same fortress-like walls and towers, the same tall belfry, and the same hospitably open gates through which we pass to visit the six separate churches of the institution, of which the prettiest is that of the five domes, called the Summer Church, while the most striking is the Winter Church, where on the day of our

THE WINTER CHURCH

visit they are holding the last service of the season; for spring has come, and it is moving day at Simonoff.

The Madonna, who throughout the winter period has been worshipped in this storm-proof basilica, must be transferred this very noon to her summer sanctuary. We are in time to witness the procession. A crowd of fanatical peasant women follow the procession from church to church, wringing their hands, and crying and sobbing as if in agony. Why they should thus bewail, as their favorite icon is carried to her most gorgeous shrine, we could not understand. The only answer inquiry brought forth was that it was a custom, but whence derived no one could tell. On arrival at the Summer Church their lamentations ceased suddenly, proving that the women were not really moved.

There is much food for the reflection of the judicious in the contrast between the poverty-stricken people who

FOLLOWING THE ICON

A VENERABLE MONK

frequent the churches and the incalculable hidden riches of
the religious orders. It would be
rash to hazard a guess as to the
value of the evangiles and
icons in the old treasury of
Simonoff ; while they are
of solid gold and silver,
these metals are com-
paratively valueless, a
mere background on
which shimmer constel-
lations of diamonds and
conflagrations of glowing
rubies and Milky Ways of

INFORMATION

ICONS

precious pearls. It can almost be believed that there are as many pearls in Russia as there are grains of sand upon her shores. In every church and monastery we see not only icons studded thick with pearls, but episcopal miters that look like sugar-loaves of pearls, and vestments —long-flowing sacerdotal robes — so stiff

ICONOSTASIS

REPOSE

with pearls embroidered into them that they can-
not be folded, and would, if stood upright on the floor, remain
erect without support, as if the spirit shapes of long-departed
priests were holding them for our inspection.

And then, in cruel contrast to this useless heaping up of
unproductive wealth, is the black, hopeless poverty of the
devout and faithful mujiks who come by hundreds bringing
their meager offerings to the monks, accepting in exchange a
bowl of soup, a slab of black bread, and a blessing. The
Russian serfs were freed in 1861 from their corporeal bond-
age, but they still wear the manacles of ignorance and
grossest superstition. It were an affront to the word
"religion" to apply it to some of the exhibitions of almost
fetish-worship of sticks and bones and tatters that I witnessed during an influx of peasant pilgrims at the Troitsa
Monastery. I am not often moved; but I confess that one

day, after looking at a mob of peasants fighting for a chance to pay for the privilege of kissing the frontal bone of some defunct old worthy laid out in a silver coffin, beside which ministers of God sat collecting fees, I turned away with tears

MUJIK PILGRIMS

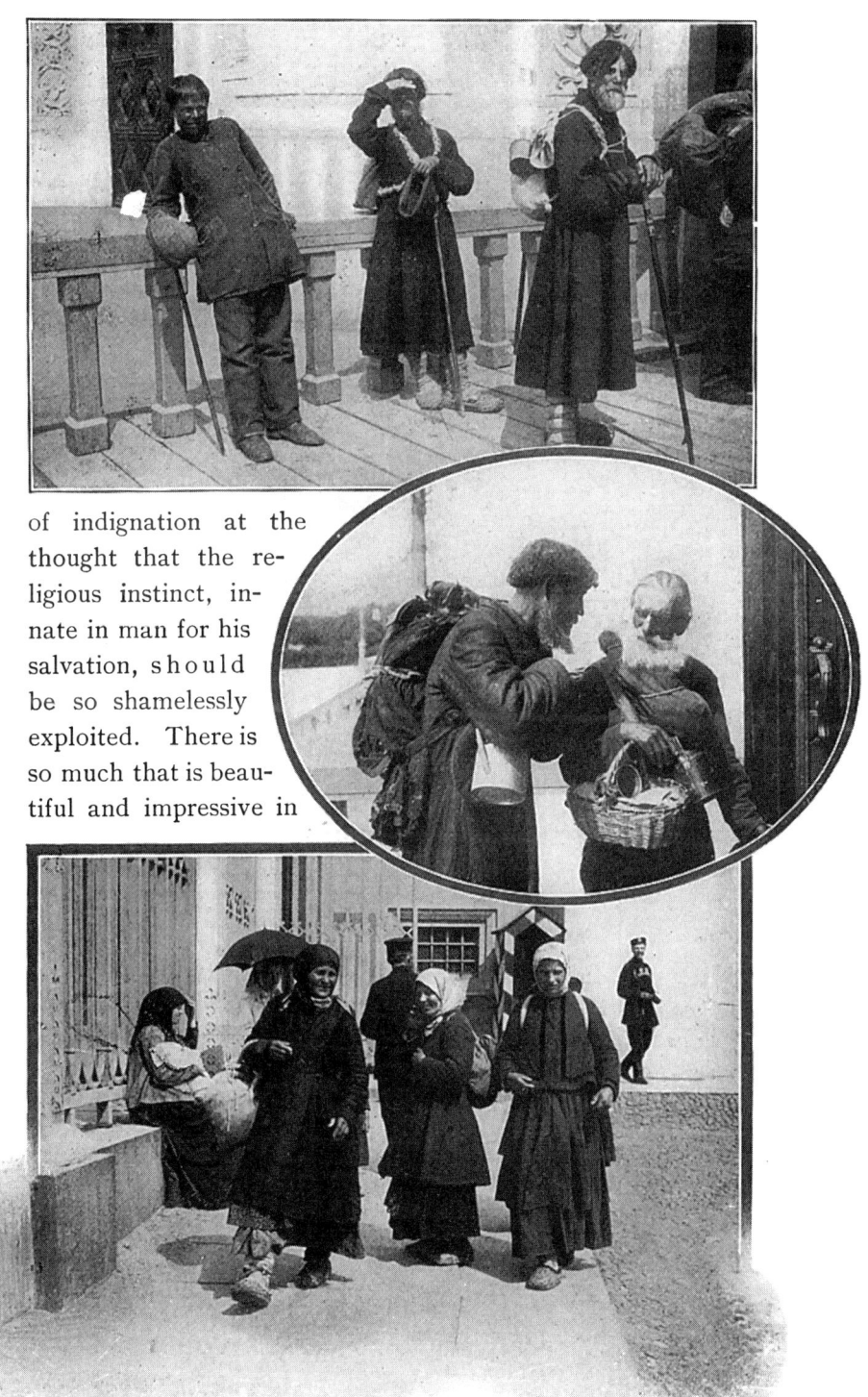

of indignation at the thought that the religious instinct, innate in man for his salvation, should be so shamelessly exploited. There is so much that is beautiful and impressive in

MUJIK PILGRIMS

the Russian form of worship, and the church is so rich that it could well afford to discourage these pitiable scenes which are painful to all intelligent witnesses, and which must grieve even those who profess the Orthodox belief. But, however we may deprecate the extravagant practices of the ignorant classes, reprehensible upon merely sanitary grounds,

WALL OF THE "CHINESE CITY"

—for the indiscriminate kissing of relics and icons must be a sure and constant means for the dissemination of disease-germs—we must confess that many of the religious expressions of the Russians denote a faith well founded and sincere.

Religion with the Russian is an affair of every day, and almost every minute of every hour in the day is he reminded by the church that something is expected of him. In the streets of Moscow are the sacred pigeons, which must be fed at the expense of pious passers-by, who buy the corn with which to feed the ever-hungry flocks from the old women stationed at various street-corners where the birds congregate. A few copecks are given; the old woman crosses herself, mutters a prayer, and tosses several handfuls of grain upon the pavement; and instantly the sky darkens as a cloud of feathered pensioners swoop down from the neighboring eaves. The pigeons are found in great numbers on the wall of the Kitai Gorod, or "Chinese City," a name that carries us back to the days of the Mongol domination of Moscow.

Of Tatar rule few evidences now remain; even the traces of the early Muscovite period have been obliterated by

HOUSE OF THE ROMANOFFS

successive conflagrations and rebuildings of the city. There is but one house left to illustrate how the Russian noblemen or Boyards lived, three hundred years ago. It is called the House of the Romanoffs, for it was the birthplace of Michael Feodorovitch, founder of the present dynasty, who became Tsar in 1613. Every detail of the domestic life led by the men who made Moscow great may be studied within these

THE FINEST PRIVATE HOUSE IN MOSCOW

walls. On the ground-floor we see the kitchen where the meats were cooked; above, the low-ceiled rooms where the lord and master of the mansion dwelt; and on the topmost floor the quarters for the women, who, as in Oriental countries, were secluded in their own apartments, known as the Terem. A glimpse of the interior reveals an atmosphere of luxury and coziness not found in modern palaces. We can imagine the comforting sense of seclusion afforded by these thick walls, microscopic windows, and low, congenial ceilings during the long, dark evenings of the northern winter, when arctic blasts beat against the dense old walls and snow swirled vainly past the narrow casements.

In the same massive style, but far more ornate and magnificent, is the modern dwelling recently constructed in another quarter by a Siberian millionaire. It is undoubtedly the finest private residence in Russia, and the most appropriate in design and execution; for it is typically Muscovite,

VASSILY-BLAJENNI

A SACRED PICTURE

and, although boasting every twentieth century convenience, is ponderously suggestive of the good old days before the perversity of Peter the Great forced on Russia an art and architecture whose productions are but composite imitations of what the imperial traveler had seen in Holland, Germany, and France. One more reminder of an architecture that is now no more is the unspeakably fantastic church of Vassily-Blajenni or St. Basil, a mendicant monk of the sixteenth century said to have been as crazy as the design of his marvelous memorial. Description falters, words lose color, phrases utterly

BENEATH ST. BASIL'S DOMES

fail to frame this structural monstrosity, so monstrous in
its ugliness that it is positively beautiful.   Every civilization and every epoch has produced its characteristic pile.
In the church of Vassily-Blajenni are distinctly typified the
civilization of the early Muscovite and the fearful reign of
Ivan the Terrible, the Nero of the Slavonic race.   Just
as Ivan's imperial torturer brought his victims to an ecstasy

THE RED SQUARE

of agony so intense that they knew not whether they were
suffering pain or pleasure, so this creation of his architect
tortures our eyes, until we exclaim in one and the same
breath, "How hideous!—how beautiful!" and know not
which expression voices our true feeling.   We know not
whether to praise or blame the Tsar Ivan, who put out the
eyes of the unhappy designer of this church lest he should
build another like it.   The interior is extremely curious.

THE TRETIAKOFF GALLERY

Tiny cells or chapels under every dome; low narrow doorways pierced in walls so thick that we can easily imagine that the church was sculptured from one gigantic block of stone, in which the little caverns and their connecting corridors had been laboriously mined and hollowed. Or, again, we have the sensation of wandering through the passages

ROUMIANTSOFF MUSEUM

IN THE RIADY

of richly frescoed catacombs. But in Moscow the medieval and the modern are everywhere face to face. Fronting on the same great square is the magnificent arcade which is called the Riady, the finest and most commodious structure of its kind in Europe, surpassing the splendid galleries in Naples and Milan. What a tremendous contrast in construction between the flat-walled and fantastic church and the light, crystal-

roofed classical Riady! It has three aisles of equal length, breadth, and height, and six transverse passages, shorter but quite as high and roomy as the longitudinal arcades. The Riady is more than a city in itself; it is almost a nation, an electric-lighted, steam-heated land to which all Moscow can resort for business and for pleasure during the long, dark winter

A MAGNIFICENT MEMORIAL

of this northern latitude, and enjoy the illusion of summer while the streets outside are blocked with snow.

The sights of Moscow are chiefly Moscow itself and the Kremlin, which we shall visit last of all ; but of course there are museums, picture-galleries, and churches that are of supreme interest. In the superb old palace of the Roumiantsoff there are ethnological collections of great interest ; across the river in the Tretiakoff Gallery is a collection of 1500 canvases, by Russian painters. But these things call for days, and we have only minutes to dispose of, and, moreover, we see in the distance something that commands attention. It is the splendid church of Christa Spasitelya, or as we would say it,

THE CHURCH OF THE HOLY SAVIOR

"Christ the Redeemer." It is usually called the church of the Holy Savior. It commemorates the saving of the fatherland from the aggressions of Napoleon in 1812. As we look upon this superb memorial, our thoughts involuntarily go back to that historic, simple monument that may be seen near Vilna in Poland. On one side of the stone there are engraved the words, "Napoleon Buonaparte passed this way in 1812, with four hundred thousand men"; and on the

PORTAL OF THE CHURCH OF THE HOLY SAVIOR

other side "Napoleon Buonaparte passed this way in 1812 with nine thousand men." The story of a tremendous tragedy never was written in fewer or more expressive words.

The original plan was to erect a great memorial upon the crest of the Sparrow Hills, whence Buonaparte first looked with triumph upon the city of his dream ; but after ten years had been devoted to the laying of foundations, Nicholas I abandoned the idea, and ordered the commencement of the

temple upon its present site, within a half-mile of the Kremlin. Begun in 1837, the edifice was finished only in 1883,
and is therefore the most modern, as well as the most splendid monument in Moscow. Variety is the spice of travel,
just as it is the spice of life. Golden domes and marble
walls and shrines of malachite, however wonderful, begin in
time to pall upon our overfeasted eyes; we cry for change

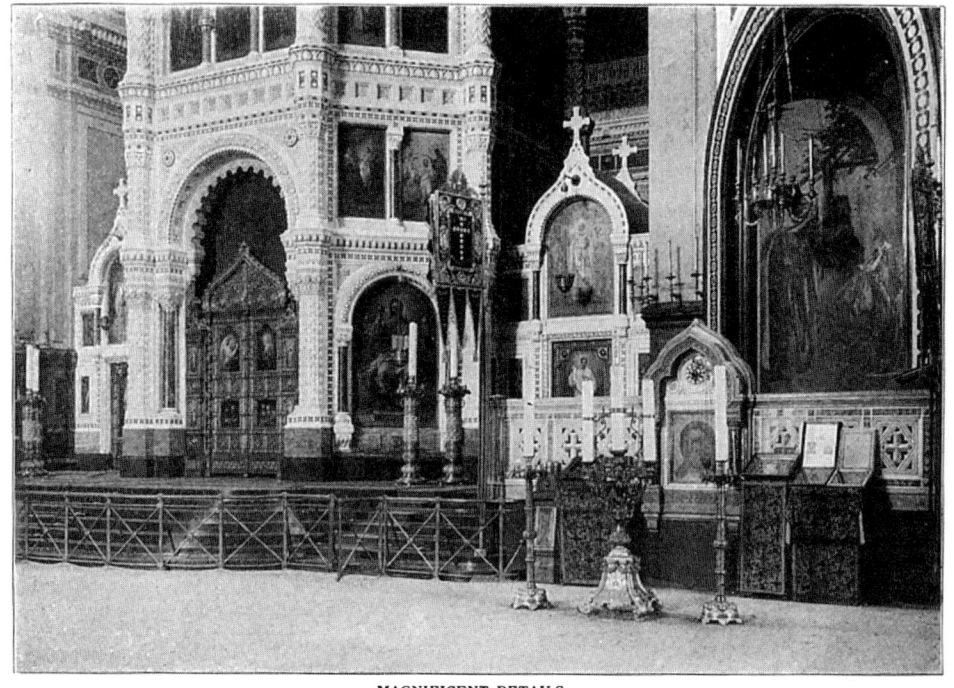

MAGNIFICENT DETAILS

and lo!—all Moscow blazes with the posters of a gorgeous
show, the first floral-parade, or *battaille de fleurs*, ever
held so near the Arctic Circle. Everybody predicted failure
for the floral fête, and people flocked by thousands to the
race-course on the day appointed, many coming with the
hope that they might see their dire predictions justified.

We fell in with the crowd, rather, we fell into the hands
of an exorbitant droski-driver, and found ourselves whirling

THE ARCH OF TRIUMPH

down the Tverskaya, out through the Arch of Triumph, now
profaned by a trolley-line, and along the suburban boulevard to the entrance of the most imposing race-course in the
world. The grand-stand is about half a mile from the outer

ENTRANCE TO THE RACE-COURSE

THE GRAND-STAND

gate. The alley leading thence was jammed with vehicles
on the day of the expected fiasco. The police at the grand-
stand had all that they could do to get the cabs and car-
riages, troïkas, and tarantasses out of the way in time to

THE GRAND DUCAL BOX

A GARDEN ON WHEELS

clear the approach for the imperial patrons of the charitable fete, the Grand Duke Sergius, Governor General of Moscow, the Grand Duchess, and their aristocratic suite.

THE BATTLE RAGES

A DAINTILY
DECORATED TRAP

After a fearful struggle at the gates we found ourselves on the course, armed with a permit from the courteous Grand Master of Police. On either side are boxes filled with the rank and fashion of the city, well provided with the floral ammunition piled high in countless baskets. The persons who had planned the fête made it a success from the artistic point of view; the skeptics who came to witness the fiasco insured an even greater triumph on the financial side. Not even Nice has ever seen a finer show than that presented by the Russian traps which first pass slowly in review, that all may observe and admire them.

A little later the battle begins and rages until nightfall. Millions of bouquets were thrown, bouquets imported from the south of France; hundreds of pretty frocks were ruined; scores of hats were badly smashed, for some of the apparently innocent

A RURAL FLOAT

projectiles were loaded, and weighed several pounds apiece. It reminded one of the palmy days upon the Riviera before the Carnival became the fixed perfunctory thing it is to-day.

This being the first time that Moscow had ever indulged in this ruinously costly, but supremely pretty pastime, the

ONE OF THE BELLES

Muscovites went mad in their enthusiasm and excitement; the padded coachmen were the only individuals impervious to the hilarity that prevailed so long as a single carriage remained upon the track. Nay, longer; for after all the original combatants had left the field strewn with ten million flowers, the crowds upon the grand-stand possessed themselves of the abandoned missiles, and carried on an infantry-battle of flowers, regiments of spectators bombarding one

FIRING FLORAL BROADSIDES

another, shouting, laughing, and screaming with merriment until at dark the police ordered them away.

We supped that evening with the fashionable mob at one of the cafés-chantants in the Petrovsky Park. Upon the edge of the suburban *"bois"* of Moscow stands a palace of red brick called the Château Petrovsky, where the Tsars are lodged when they come to Moscow to be crowned, and

THE CHÂTEAU PETROVSKY

LOOKING TOWARD THE KHODYNSKY POLÉ

whither they retire after their ceremony at the Kremlin. But Nicholas did not return thither after his coronation in 1896. We know full well why he holds and will ever hold this place in horror, for its windows command the fatal field called the Khodynsky Polé, scene of that awful tragedy of the coronation crush, when thousands of helpless peasants crowded themselves to death or mutilation in their eagerness to taste the bounty of the Tsar, and to receive imperial souvenirs. No one will ever know just how it came about or just what happened. Three hundred thousand men, women, and children of the poorer class were gathered together here, peasant pilgrims from many provinces, most of that multitude having slept upon the field that they might

SCENE OF THE CORONATION CRUSH

be at hand for the promised free distribution of food, drink, and coronation-cups. At daybreak the still poorer populace of Moscow rolled its unruly tide of festive misery out from the back streets and alleys of the industrial quarters, all surging toward a common center, around which were already massed a quarter of a million people. Tighter and tighter grew the press, until those acres of serried humanity began to sway and roll like an awakened sea under the stress of sudden

THE MOSCOW HOME OF TOLSTOI

gusts of terror. Madness then took possession of the mob, and, helpless in its immensity, it ground out the lives of fourteen hundred of its atoms and maimed and mutilated many thousands more. Meantime, at the Kremlin, Nicholas, stepping before a gathering of earthly royalties, placed the great crown of all the Russias on his head, and swore in the hearing of the King of Kings that he would save, protect, and uplift the people confided to his care. But no blame can attach to the Tsar for the catastrophe. The blinded, ignorant multitude that did itself to death but typifies the helplessness of strength and numbers when left without the rudder of intelligence and cut loose from the anchor of authority. Till Russia's masses shall, through the slow beneficent influences of education, become intelligent, the safety of the nation lies

THE HOTEL AT TOULA

in absolute autocracy. This consideration may throw new light upon some of the problems discussed by Russian reformers and their foreign critics. Suppose the dream of Tolstoi to be at once realized in Russia. Disband the army, muster out the costly corps of police, abolish courts of law, — even law itself, — give absolute independence of thought and action to the hundred million souls who have not learned to think or act, and the Russian masses, like the vast multitude that trampled down the victims of the coronation crush, would inevitably annihilate thousands in the terrible maëlstrom of a national catastrophe.

My sympathies have ever been with the cause of industrial emancipation, and therefore with Tolstoi, for he is one of the great champions of liberty ; but my reason, so far as

ON THE WAY TO TOLSTOI'S COUNTRY-SEAT

the Russia of the present is concerned, must render a decision in accord with the Tsar, and with his conservative ministers.

The home of Count Tolstoi in Moscow is an unpretentious dwelling, to which we sent our guide, one day, to ask if the count would see us if we should call. The servants told the guide that the count was out. He was ; for as our

TOLSTOI'S FRONTIER

emissary turned away, he saw the aged writer issuing from another door to take a carriage. In a very few words he

THE GATE OF YASNAYA POLIANA

THE VILLAGERS

stated his mission. The count replied in this oracular fashion : "I am not at home to all the world ; above all I am not
at home for interviews ; but an American can always find me."

A DRAM-SHOP

But to find Count Tolstoi is, even for an American, a thing easier said than done ; for before we could accept the invitation, or challenge, to seek him out, he had left Moscow and retired to his country-seat, Yasnaya Poliana, near the town of Toula.   But, not discouraged, we gladly undertook a six-hour railway journey to Toula and a carriage-drive of fifteen versts to the estate of the " grand old man " of Russia.

THE VILLAGE STREET

We arrived at half-past eight in the morning ; for believing that Count Tolstoi, despite his great age, seventy-two years, was still leading the life of a peasant farmer, we thought the hour none too early.   But no one was astir except a servant.   We wait for an hour and a half, driving through the adjacent village, peopled by the folk whose fathers were the serfs of the Tolstoi estate.   Rank misery pervades the filthy and disgusting village-settlement, no better and no worse than villages in other parts of Russia. A deformed woman and a big strapping mujik are insistent in their demands for money, and servile in their thanks upon receiving it. As we gaze about us, we strive in vain to reconcile the altruistic theories of the master and the existent conditions in this village at his gates.

At ten o'clock we again present ourselves at the count's door. His eldest son, who bears the father's name,

COUNT TOLSTOI'S SUMMER VILLA

received us kindly with the words, "Father will be here presently." Meantime we have observed, beneath a tree near the door, three peasant women waiting patiently; they were waiting there when we came first, two hours earlier. At last they seem to wake; they rise expectantly as an old man in mujik costume steps briskly down from the veranda. It is Count Leo Tolstoi, one of the world's great men.

A hurried greeting to us, a fatherly smile to Leo, Jr., and the count begs our indulgence for a moment, saying as he turns toward the old peasant women under the tree, "You must excuse me. These poor women first. They have had a fire in their village; three times they have had a fire; they have lost many things and I must speak to them." It is all perfectly sincere and beautiful; but—cynics that we are—we think how marvelously effective it all is from the dramatic point of view: The waiting pensioners beneath the ancestral tree; the aged lord of the manor, who, though a nobleman, is clad in the dress of the poor mujik, hastily courteous to his foreign guests, but most concerned with the misfortunes of the native poor who await him.

A SAGE IN PEASANT GARB

Tolstoi speaks English fluently, but with an accent that suggests the speech of Henry Irving, with an added Gallic twist. He talks upon a dozen subjects with equal interest, enthusiasm, and, above all, originality. There should be no law ; no man should have the right to judge or to condemn another ; absolute freedom of the individual is the only thing that will redeem the world. Christ was a great teacher, nothing more. This was the sum and substance of his views as expressed to my companion, a distinguished American, in June, 1901. But Tolstoi both claims and exercises the right

"MY GRANDCHILDREN"

to revise opinions, and proclaims from time to time a new and always startling attitude toward the truths and contentions in the great arena of philosophic thought.

We breakfasted with him on the veranda, a large and loving family gathered round the samovar ; the two dainty grandchildren relieved with the note of youth and hope and freshness the almost sad impression produced upon us by the atmosphere of neglect and tumble-downness permeating

not only the peasant village but even the house and private
grounds of the estate, of which the Russian title, ''Yasnaya
Poliana'' means the Bright Plain, or the Illuminated Field.
Even if we cannot sympathize with the almost fatalistic
philosophy of a return to nature — a philosophy that would
let all things go to seed, we are not blind to the brightness
that illumines the Yasnaya Poliana, for it is the brightness of

WHERE THE WATERS OF THE MOSKVA ARE BLESSED

a mighty mind, an intellectual luminosity that has lighted for
all time the dark path trodden by oppressed humanity.

Such, in brief, were the reflections brought back to Moscow
from the home of him whose name is better known throughout
the world than that of any other Russian save that of the Tsar
himself, — the Tsar, who stands for all the old sage condemns.
who is defender of the faith that Tolstoi has assailed, that Russian faith of which the Kremlin is the most sacred stronghold.

SHRINE OF AN ICON

Around the towers of the Kremlin cluster the religious aspirations of the Slavonic people to whom religion and worship are things of daily, hourly concern.

In all the busy thoroughfares we find, crowded in between the shops, small chapels or the shrines of celebrated icons, each one demanding recognition, offerings, salutations. Rarely does a Muscovite pass any of the eleven hundred chapels without uncovering and signing himself, while many stop to pray or enter to deposit an offering.

The most famous of these icons is the Iberian Madonna, housed in a chapel at the gate to the Red Square. It is a picture of the Virgin, copied by fasting monks from a most sacred portrait in one of the monasteries of Mount Athos in the Ægean Sea. It was sent as a gift to the Orthodox Tsars of Moscow in 1648. The present emperor, when he comes to Moscow, drives directly to this gate that he may offer prayers to the most sacred icon in his most sacred city. All day the faithful throng the little chapel. As the French guide-book says, "*La chapelle est habituellement pleine,*" and then, in parentheses, "*prendre garde aux pickpockets.*

But the Madonna is rarely at home by day; her visitors see and kiss only a substituted copy; for she must make her daily round of visits to the houses where pious souls have called to her from sick-beds — or where she is expected to bless with her presence some joyful ceremony, — a wedding or a christening. For each of these visits she receives from twenty-five to a hundred dollars, and therefore can afford to ride in grander state than the humble rival icon, whose neglected shrine is near at hand, and whose more modest coach is shown in an illustration. Unfortunately, we failed to secure pictures of the equipage of the Iberian Icon. Day after day we lay in wait in vain; she always came home too late in the day for picture-making. Her state-carriage is drawn by

THE IBERIAN CHAPEL

six horses, with driver and postilion in brilliant livery, but bareheaded. Her progress through the streets is like that of an empress. All traffic ceases, every head is bared and bowed, all hands wave the outline of the cross, all lips are moved in prayer; and when, upon arrival, the huge gilded frame is carried from the coach, we see scores of men, women, and children throw themselves upon their knees and crawl frantically toward it, frequently doing one another

WORSHIPERS

bodily injury in the attempt to kiss the sides, the back, the corners, or any available surface of the bejeweled thing. Meantime, by way of striking contrast, we saw the attendants sitting in the coach calmly counting over the day's receipts in a most businesslike and public fashion.

Another famous icon is Our Lady of Vladimir, whose throne is in the holiest of the Kremlin churches, where the Tsars are crowned. When she goes forth to spend the day at chapels or churches in the city proper, she is accompanied

WORSHIPERS

by the high clergy, including even the Metropolitan of
Moscow, and scores of religious societies, composed of

THE EQUIPAGE OF AN ICON

several thousand volunteers, who carry in her train the weighty golden banners, which during her sojourn are stacked for blocks along the shop-fronts in all the streets adjacent to the chapel she has honored with a call.

We witnessed the passing of her escort as she returned with pageantry and pomp and splendor to her Kremlin home. It is no easy matter, even for a half-dozen sturdy Russians to

"OUR LADY OF VLADIMIR IS WITHIN"

hold unswervingly aloft those flags of solid metal, loaded with gems and precious stones. Frequent were the stoppages of the procession, ludicrous the efforts of the bearers to appear at ease when threatened with the downfall of a banner. Hundreds and hundreds of devoted banner-bearers filed past us, staggering under the weight of sanctified insignia. At last comes the bright yellow river of the clergy, robed in vestments of cloth of gold. Behind this regiment of

SACRED INSIGNIA

holy men are borne the sacred relics from the Kremlin, and the great picture of the Vladimir Madonna, whose history,

TROUBLE WITH A BANNER

it has been said, is the history of Russia. Her golden frame is valued at one hundred thousand dollars, the emerald upon her brow is worth the ransom of a prince. Behind her walks the highest dignitary of the Russian Church, the aged Metropolitan of Moscow, and on all sides stand or kneel the throngs of bareheaded poor, looking with awe and wonder upon this living stream of gold that flows in long waves of glittering splendor through the hushed and silent streets.

THE PROCESSION

We follow the procession to the Gate of the Redeemer, most sacred portal of the Kremlin, above which hangs a picture of the Savior, to which all passers-by must pay a reverential homage. No Russian ever passes through the gate without uncovering his head; in fact, the taking off of hats was formerly enforced by law, and is to-day enforced by custom — stronger than any legal regulation.

The gate dates from the end of the fifteenth century. The lower part was built by an Italian architect. The spire was added by an Englishman after a lapse of a hundred and thirty-five years. The other towers and walls are of equal age and equally impressive. The circuit of the walls is greater than one mile, and there are five great gates, each dominated by a tower. We enter with bared heads through

THE REDEEMER GATE

the Redeemer's Portal, finding ourselves in a surprisingly vast level square, above which rises the most famous edifice in Russia. It is the belfry of the Kremlin, known as the tower of Ivan Veliky. It marks the very heart of Russia. Within the circle of its shadow lie the holiest shrines of Muscovy: the cathedral in which the Tsars are crowned, another where Imperial marriages are solemnized, and a third in which the Tsars of old sleep their last sleep, content to rest forever in the city where they ruled, while their successors slumber in still another, new necropolis, upon the banks of the cold Neva in modern St. Petersburg.

In the shadow of the tower are two famous and familiar things; one is a cannon, the other is a bell. In front of the *caserne* is ranged

THE NICHOLAS GATE

KREMLIN RAMPARTS

IVAN'S TOWER

a battery of picturesque old cannon, of which the biggest and
most ornamental and most ridiculously useless is the so-called
"Tsar of the Cannon" of the Kremlin.   The thirteen-inch
guns of modern warfare seem mere bean-blowers in compari-
son with this stumpy thunderer which takes a ball measur-
ing one meter in diameter.   But unfortunately this piece of
ordnance cannot project these 39-inch balls without endan-
gering its own integrity and also that of the entire Kremlin.
Equally impressive, although voiceless also, is the Tsar of
Bells, the hugest in the
world, weighing two hun-
dred tons.   The bell was
cast in 1735, but was not
taken from the mold until
two years later, before
which time, unhappily, a
conflagration cracked off

THE TSAR OF CANNON

A HISTORIC FRAGMENT

a fragment nearly seven feet in height, and robbed the mighty bronze of the deep voice that might have been to-day one of the supreme sound sensations of the world. That fragment has a fascination for every passer-by ; it is worn glossy by the touch of sympathetic hands, which every day caress it curiously. No one seems able to resist the attraction of this magnet ; —warmed by the sun, it offers to every touch an almost human

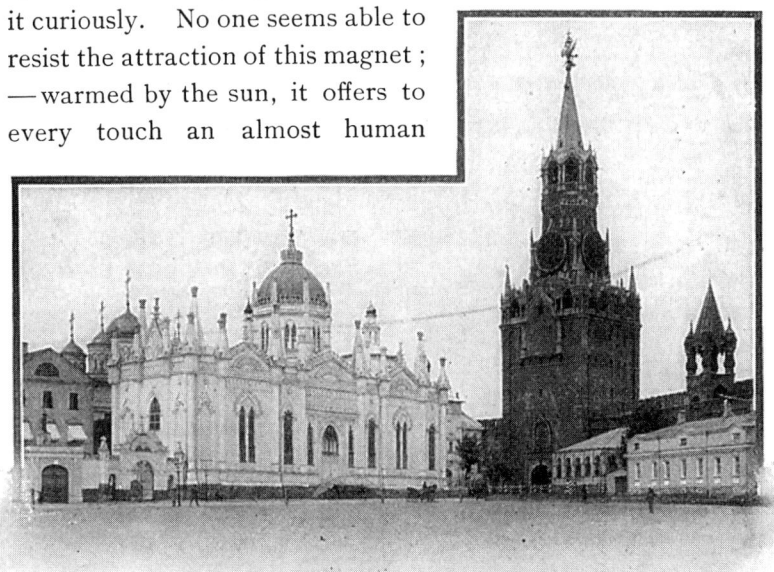

CONVENT OF THE ASCENSION AND THE REDEEMER GATE

contact, as if a little of the life of all the millions who have
fondled it had in some mysterious way passed into this mass
of bronze and made of it a sentient, responsive thing.

Gazing almost directly at this shattered stillborn metal
dome is the bronze image of a Tsar, whose useful life was
tragically ended by the Nihilists twenty years ago.   It is a
strange fatality that both of the great emancipators should

THE BELL, THE TOWER, THE SYNOD, AND THE CANNON

have perished at the hand of an assassin ; yet our Lincoln,
the president who freed the slaves in the new world, and
Alexander, the tsar who gave liberty to the Russian serfs,
alike fell victims to the fury of political fanatics.

A new memorial to Alexander II has been but recently
completed.   Modern in its magnificence, it fortunately har-
monizes with the medieval splendors that surround it.   It
both dignifies and graces the noble brow of the sacred

Kremlin Hill. The statue itself is a perfect likeness of the man who, had he lived, would have given a constitution to the Russian people. The manner of his violent death convinced those who succeeded him in government that Russia was not ripe for liberty.

So it has always been and ever will be. The regicide, the killer of the man in power, can do naught but injure and disgrace the cause he thinks to serve, the noblest cause for which man ever fought — the cause of human liberty. The calm, superb, robed figure of the murdered Tsar, with its outstretched hand, that in the one gesture seems to bless and to protest, is a perpetual witness to the futility of violence. The ranks of law and order, no matter how breached and decimated, al-

IMPERAL ROBES IN BRONZE

ways reform in serried resolute array; new workers take the places of the old, new captains do not fear to take up the succession and the responsibilities of the leaders who have fallen.

The Kremlin, to be literal, the "Citadel," or the inner enceinte of Moscow, is a city in itself, but we have time for only a brief

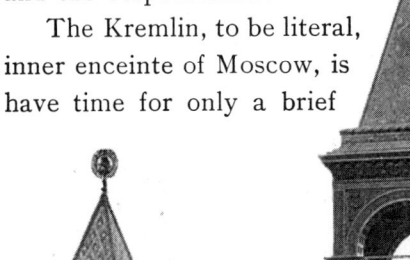

MONUMENT OF ALEXANDER II

ONE OF THE OLD GUARD

review of the chief edifices of this remarkable enclosure. Let us begin with the largest, though not the most important, the Palace of Justice, upon which glitters in golden characters the word "*Zakon*," "L a w." Facing it is the Arsenal, with the word "Victory," not expressed in letters but almost shouted by the mouths of eight hundred and seventy-five captured cannon— chiefly souvenirs of Napoleon's disastrous visit in 1812. Another large, comparatively modern pile is the Grand Palace of the Tsars, vast and to-day unoccupied, which was the scene of splendid ceremonies on the occasion of the coronation in 1896. Adjoining it is a museum that contains the thrones and vestments used by the imperial personages who have been

THE PALACE OF JUSTICE AND THE ARSENAL

THE KREMLIN FROM THE WEST

PANORAMA OF THE KREMLIN

THE GRAND PALACE OF THE KREMLIN

crowned in Moscow. The robes and diadems of Nicholas
and Alix are already catalogued and placed on view behind

By permission

THRONE ROOM IN THE KREMLIN PALACE

IN THE GRAND PALACE OF THE KREMLIN

plate-glass, as if the wearers were already dead and gone, as if they were already members of the vanished company whose dresses, finery, and baubles are exposed in other cases.   Just beyond the palace stands the Church of the Annunciation, where of old the imperial folk were united to the church by baptism, and to one another in the bonds of holy wedlock.   Its domes and roofs are golden ; its walls covered with frescoed nightmares ; its pavement made of blocks of jasper, presented by a Shah of Persia many years ago.   Facing the same enclosure is the Church of the Archangel, where Peter's predecessors sleep amid the dust of ages and the wealth of

A KREMLIN SENTRY

GRANOVITAYA PALATA

WHERE TSARS ARE BAPTIZED AND MARRIED

Orthodoxy ; and on another side is the headquarters of the Holy Synod, which controls the mighty religious machinery of the Orthodox church.   But the most important structure is the square, five-domed cathedral of the Assumption, within which every Tsar of Russia has been crowned, or rather has himself placed the crown upon his own imperial brow.   We were struck by the spectacle that greeted us within. The space

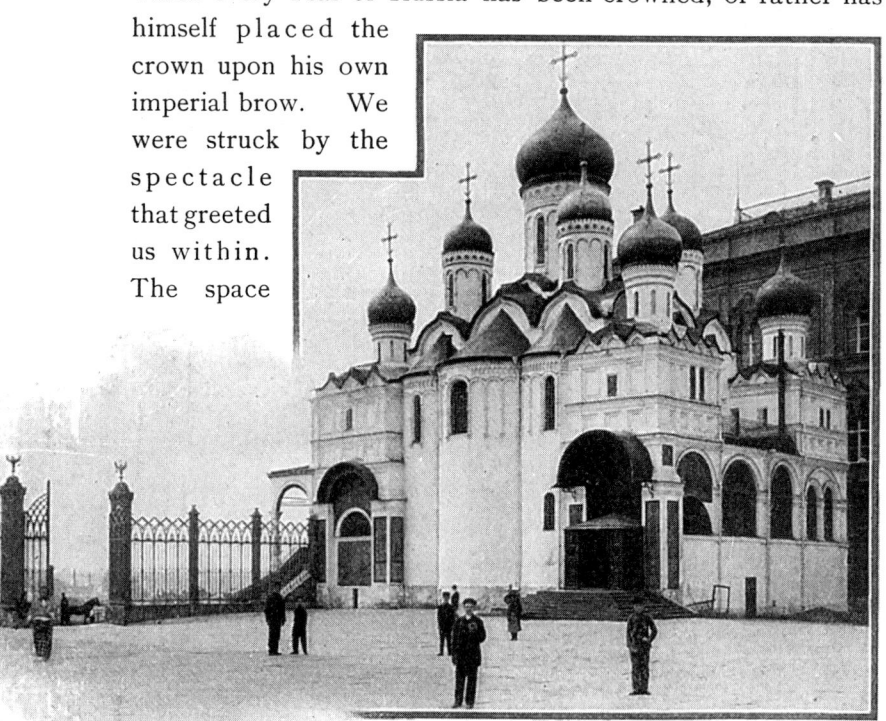

CATHEDRAL OF THE ANNUNCIATION

within the four great central columns was securely hedged about with ropes and carpeted with gorgeous rugs.   Five or six officials in full-dress uniforms were standing there engaged in ceremonial worship, while on the altar terrace and in the holy of holies beyond the iconostasis a score of superbly groomed and gorgeously arrayed priests and bishops were chanting with wonderful bass voices, organ-like in their sonority, the music of the mass.   And then, to complete the interesting picture, there stood outside the ropes, in the

A MEDIEVAL HALL OF THE KREMLIN

narrow space around the walls, at least a thousand humble, devout, and rudely-clad pilgrims and poor folk, smelling of poverty and toil, but breathing devotion, looking awe, and thinking we know not what. They were so thick that they stood on one another's toes; literally, there was not standing-room, while just beyond the ropes, against which they scarcely dared to press, stood the half-dozen glittering functionaries, each one disposing of four times more space than had been left for the respectful, patient mob that looked on, prayed, and crowded itself and thanked its stars that it had been allowed even to cross the threshold.

Half smothered, we retreated from the crowded church, and climbed the winding stairs of Ivan's Tower. A vision of surpassingly fantastic charm greets us as we halt and gaze out through a window. Domes, spires, towers, and pinnacles and pyramids, and then still other domes and spires, until the eye fails to distinguish more, and the imagination must be called upon to fill in all the distant details of the picture. Immediately below us is the red Convent of the Miracles, the richest in all Russia, with domes of a marvelous blue. Beyond it is another convent, with its dome-crowned Churches, then the Redeemer Gate, and beyond that, Moscow itself, which means an infinity of other domes and towers. Mounting still higher we look toward the south, toward the great Church of the Redeemer and the Sparrow Hills. The Moskva River creeps below the Kremlin walls, whispering to him who has ears for its tremendous story, the secrets of a troubled past — the tale of Moscow's rise to power — of the evolution of the "Mother city" of the Russians from the palisaded fort erected on this hill by rude Slavonic men nine centuries ago. It tells of the dark days of Mongol domination, of struggle, rebellion, and final victory over the Tatar horde, — of the first man who claimed the

By permission

MUSCOVITE LUXURY

DOMES AND TOWERS

title Tsar, Ivan IV, surnamed Terrible ; — then Peter is the next name murmured — almost reproachfully, by the Moskva waves, for it was Peter who robbed Moscow of her imperial

By permission

A KREMLIN COUCH

glory and transferred the capital to Petersburg ;—then in exultant undertones the stream rehearses the tragic story of the French invasion, how Napoleon came with a mighty host, how the invader saw the sacred city vanish like a smoking sacrifice upon the altar of the fatherland, and then how he withdrew, a conquered conqueror, along that bitter pathway marked throughout its dreadful length in the Russian snow by the frozen forms of Frenchmen.

CATHEDRAL OF THE ASSUMPTION

Well may the tower of Ivan stir the soul of every Russian !—for it defied the man who had defied the world. Its bells sounded the first notes of the death-knell of Napoleon. Well may it command the love and reverence of every faithful Muscovite, for it stands upon the holiest ground in Russia, marking the very cradle of the Empire of the Slav. Well may he look upon it with satisfied and yet insatiate ambition

IN THE CATHEDRAL OF THE ASSUMPTION

as he recalls the fact that once upon a time the stretch of country visible from its summit was all that could be claimed as the appanage of the Princes of Muscovy, while to-day the broad dominion of the Muscovite Tsar embraces the vaster parts of two great continents; and, though the eye of the Russian is

WHERE TSARS ARE CROWNED

CONVENT OF THE MIRACLES

not able to reach so far, his hand, first outstretched from
the Kremlin merely to repel the Tatar hordes, now holds the

LOOKING EAST FROM IVAN'S TOWER

half of Europe, the half of Asia, touches the frozen Arctic, the sunny Black Sea and the Caspian, the Baltic and the Japan Sea ; has gripped at Vladivostok the safest and most beautiful harbor in the Farthest East; is now caressing with insidious intent the Central Asian states on the frontier of British India. The Muscovite standing .upon the top of Ivan's Tower no longer utters the cry with which his fathers drove the Mongols forth, "Russia for the Russians!"

THE HEART OF RUSSIA

which is the cry of a young nation struggling merely for its life and for recognition. No. To-day the patriotic and far-seeing Russian — gazing with prophetic eye half-way around the globe, across two continents, across the boundless territories of Siberia, —

IVAN VELIKY

voices the new ambition of his race in the tremendous words,
"The world for Russia!"

RUSSIA

THOU dread Colossus of the North! astride
Two continents that link the East and West,
One foot on the Pacific's margin pressed,
One planted by the Baltic's icy tide ;
The laws of Nature and of man defied ;
Patient — thy heart's ambitions unconfessed ;
Binding with bands of steel each new acquest,—
Door after door, thy golden key throws wide.
Yet when the nations furiously rage,
Thine is the voice that bids them Christ's words heed!
True to thy Muscovitish heritage,—
Masking with courteous smiles insatiate greed.
"Russia for Russians!" blazed thy life's first page.
"The world for Russia!" now thine unwrit creed!

               — *Frances Bartlett*

FURTHER READING

Russia (1995), a 60-minute videocassette issued by International Video Network, contains excellent film footage of Moscow and its environs. Another excellent reference work is Brian Moynahan's *The Russian Century* (1994). This is a wonderful photographic history of Russia. Another beautifully illustrated volume is Peter Kurth's *Tsar: The World of Nicholas and Alexandra* (1995).

Anyone who wishes to find out about the major events and personalities of Europe between 1875 and 1914 should read Eric Hobsbawn's *The Age of Empire: 1875-1914* (1989). Other interesting books on the period include *Europe 1815-1914* by Gordon Craig; James Joll's *Europe Since 1870*; and *A Survey of European Civilization* (Vol. II, from 1660), by Wallace K. Ferguson and Geoffrey Brown. See also: Barbara Tuchman, *The Proud Tower* (1966); Edward R. Tannenbaum, *1900: The Generation Before the Great War* (1976); and *War by Timetable: How the First World War Began* (1969), *The Struggle for Mastery in Europe, 1848-1918* (1971), and *The Last of Old Europe: A Grand Tour* (1976), by A. J. P. Taylor.

—Dr. Fred L. Israel

CONTRIBUTORS

General Editor FRED L. ISRAEL is an award-winning historian. He received the Scribe's Award from the American Bar Association for his work on the Chelsea House series *The Justices of the United States Supreme Court.* A specialist in American history, he was general editor for Chelsea's *1897 Sears Roebuck Catalog.* Dr. Israel has also worked in association with Arthur M. Schlesinger, jr. on many projects, including *The History of U.S. Presidential Elections* and *The History of U.S. Political Parties.* He is senior consulting editor on the Chelsea House series *Looking into the Past: People, Places, and Customs,* which examines past traditions, customs, and cultures of various nations.

Senior Consulting Editor ARTHUR M. SCHLESINGER, JR. is the preeminent American historian of our time. He won the Pulitzer Prize for his book *The Age of Jackson* (1945), and again for *A Thousand Days* (1965). This chronicle of the Kennedy Administration also won a National Book Award. He has written many other books, including a multi-volume series, *The Age of Roosevelt.* Professor Schlesinger is the Albert Schweitzer Professor of Humanities at the City University of New York, and has been involved in several other Chelsea House projects, including the *American Statesmen* series of biographies on the most prominent figures in early American history.

IRVING WALLACE (1916-1990), whose essay on Burton Holmes is reprinted in the forward to The World 100 Years Ago, is one of the most widely read authors in the world. His books have sold over 200 million copies, and his best-sellers include *The Chapman Report, The Prize, The Man, The Word, The Second Lady,* and *The Miracle.*

INDEX